The Beginner's Guide to
CANDY MAKING

Inspiring | Educating | Creating | Entertaining

Brimming with creative inspiration, how-to projects, and useful information to enrich your everyday life, quarto.com is a favorite destination for those pursuing their interests and passions.

First Published in 2022 by New Shoe Press, an imprint of The Quarto Group, 100 Cummings Center, Suite 265-D, Beverly, MA 01915, USA.
T (978) 282-9590 F (978) 283-2742 Quarto.com

New Shoe Press titles are also available at discount for retail, wholesale, promotional, and bulk purchase. For details, contact the Special Sales Manager by email at specialsales@quarto.com or by mail at The Quarto Group, Attn: Special Sales Manager, 100 Cummings Center, Suite 265-D, Beverly, MA 01915, USA.

ISBN: 978-0-7603-7963-9
eISBN: 978-0-7603-7964-6

The content in this book was previously published in The Sweet Book of Candy Making (Quarry Books 2012) by Elizabeth LaBau

Library of Congress Cataloging-in-Publication Data available

Photography: Winnie Poon Ma / style.shoot.eat

The Beginner's Guide to
CANDY MAKING

ELIZABETH LABAU

Simple and Sweet Recipes for Chocolates, Caramels, Lollypops, Gummies, and More

NEW SHOE PRESS

Contents

Introduction

Some children collect baseball cards. Others collect dolls. When I was a child, I collected candy.

Every Halloween, I insisted on using an old pillowcase to gather my candy instead of a novelty candy bucket, because the pillowcase could hold so much more loot. It was thrilling to watch my candy collection grow as I roamed the neighborhood trick-or-treating, and I wouldn't stop knocking on doors until I could barely lift the pillowcase from the ground. After I shuffled home, hunched under the weight of my haul, I would carefully hide the candy in my room and hoard it like a miser for months. My goal was always to make it last until Easter, when I would receive a fresh supply of sweets.

Now that I am an adult, I have a greater appreciation for dark chocolate and less of a fondness for guzzling straight sugar, but not much else has changed. I still have an unapologetic love of candy, and if someone were to hand me a pillowcase full of chocolate today, I would gladly, gleefully, accept.

Fortunately, I am no longer dependent on the kindness of strangers to replenish my candy supply. In my job as a recipe developer, I am lucky enough to be able to make my own candy whenever a craving strikes. The basic thrill of simply eating sugar has been replaced by the joy of working with sugar to invent my own candy creations, and I hope to share this same joy with you.

Making candy at home is a magical process. Even after years of experience, it is still amazing to me that simply boiling a few ingredients together can produce luminous lollipops, and that whisking cream and chocolate together can yield soft, rich truffles. If you are new to candy making, some steps might seem intimidating, but I want to assure you that not only is it possible to make gorgeous, delicious, professional-quality candies in your home kitchen, but it is also fun.

Whether you are an experienced candy maker looking for new ideas and inspiration or a novice seeking a step-by-step candy-making guide, there is something in this book for you. Part I covers candy basics, beginning in chapter 1 with an introduction to common candy ingredients and candy-making equipment. Chapter 2 will take you through some of the fundamental techniques for working with sugar and chocolate, like how to properly boil sugar and how to temper chocolate. You may be tempted to skip this chapter to get to the recipes faster—resist! Knowing these skills is crucial to candy-making success, and it is important to be comfortable with them.

Part II is where you'll find the recipes for everything from sugar candies to caramels, chocolates to marshmallows, toffees to truffles. I have included a mix of classic recipes and contemporary flavor combinations that are meant to get you started and spur your own imagination. As you master the basic techniques and foundational elements of each recipe, I hope you will be inspired to experiment with variations and create your own unique candy combinations.

Each recipe chapter also has a troubleshooting section that addresses common problems with that type of candy, and offers solutions. In my years of candy making I have had just about every kitchen failure you can imagine, and I probably even invented a few new ones. Making a failed batch of candy can be frustrating, and I want to save you from that same fate by pointing out potential trouble areas and typical mistakes.

Finally, when you are an expert candy maker, the only thing left is to gild the lily—or the chocolate, as it were—with fancy decorating techniques! Part III offers a variety of decorating ideas for creating beautiful and unique truffles, caramels, marshmallows, and more. There are also recipes that use sugar and chocolate skills from previous chapters to make edible garnishes like spun sugar and chocolate bowls.

After you have spent time cooking from this book, I hope you will be inspired to grab your metaphorical pillowcase and fill it with candy recipes you love and want to add to your personal collection!

PART I

Getting Started

CHAPTER 1

Ingredients and Candy-Making Equipment

Ingredients

One of the easiest things you can do to ensure excellent candies is to use fresh, quality ingredients. Before you clutch your wallet in horror, understand that quality does not necessarily equate to the most expensive gourmet foods. Choosing good ingredients can be as simple as knowing the most suitable types of butter and cream to buy, when to use fresh versus frozen fruit, and the optimal chocolate for your recipe of choice. This section will introduce you to the most common candy ingredients and make a few purchasing recommendations when appropriate.

Sweeteners

Granulated sugar Granulated sugar is the product most people think of when they hear the word "sugar." Also known as white sugar or table sugar, it is the most common ingredient in candy making. It is made by refining the sweet juice from sugar cane or, increasingly, beets, into fine white crystals. Sugar that is made from pure sugar cane is usually labeled "cane sugar," but sugar that is made from beets or a combination of beet and cane sugars is often unspecified and simply called "sugar." I am a cane sugar purist—in my experience, beet sugar does not behave predictably and can produce inconsistent, undesirable results when cooked to high temperatures. I recommend buying only sugar that is clearly labeled as coming from sugar cane.

Brown sugar Brown sugar is actually granulated sugar that has molasses added back in after processing. Brown sugar is available in light and dark varieties; light brown sugar, which has a milder flavor, should be used to make the recipes

in this book. When measuring brown sugar by volume, always pack it tightly into the measuring cup to get an accurate measurement.

Powdered sugar Also known as confectioners' sugar or icing sugar, powdered sugar is made from finely pulverized granulated sugar. It often contains a small amount of cornstarch to prevent clumping. Because it easily absorbs moisture from the air, it should always be stored in an airtight container and be sifted before use to remove any lumps.

Corn syrup Corn syrup has developed a bad reputation. It is true that high-fructose corn syrup has unnecessarily weaseled its way into many packaged foods, but in my opinion corn syrup still has a place in the candy maker's kitchen. It is an invaluable tool that prevents crystallization in sugar candies, and it improves the texture of fudges and truffles. Corn syrup comes in two varieties, light and dark corn syrup. Light corn syrup is more refined and has no discernible flavor, while dark corn syrup has an amber color and a caramel taste. The two are not interchangeable, and all of the recipes in this book call for light corn syrup.

Honey Honey is a natural sweetener with a flavor that can range from light and fruity to intensely dark and pungent. You should use any honey whose flavor you enjoy eating plain, but be aware that the stronger varieties may overpower other ingredients in the candy. Make sure you use liquid honey, as opposed to the "creamed" variety.

Maple syrup Maple syrup is made from the sweet sap of the maple tree. It comes in various grades, which indicate the color and strength of the syrup. Grade A is lighter and has a more delicate flavor, while Grade B is stronger and more assertive. The variety you use is entirely dependent on your personal preference. Make sure you select genuine maple syrup as opposed to imitation "pancake syrup," which is merely a sugary syrup with maple flavoring added.

Molasses Molasses is a thick syrup with a dark color and a strong, distinctive flavor. Varieties include light molasses, dark molasses, and black-strap molasses. It should only be used in candies where you desire a molasses taste, because it can quickly overwhelm other flavors.

Artificial sweeteners There are many artificial sweeteners on the market, but none of them are suitable substitutes for sugar in candy making, and they should not be used in the recipes in this book.

Chocolates

Cocoa butter Cocoa butter is the fat that is derived from cocoa beans. It is solid at room temperature, and is commonly sold in bar or chip form. Although "cocoa butter" sounds delicious, it usually has a neutral flavor because it has been deodorized. Because cocoa butter is the same fat that is in chocolate, it can easily be added to melted chocolate to make it more fluid. It also makes an appearance in Part III, on page 129, where it is mixed with luster dust and used to paint chocolate candies.

Unsweetened chocolate As the name implies, unsweetened chocolate has no sugar added, so it is very bitter when tasted on its own. It is sometimes labeled "baking chocolate" because it is often used in baking recipes like brownies and cakes. In candy making, unsweetened chocolate is used to provide a strong chocolate flavor in recipes like fudge, which already contains a great deal of sugar from other sources.

Dark chocolate Dark chocolate is a catchall term that refers to any chocolate that contains cocoa solids, cocoa butter, and sugar, but no milk solids. Depending on the cocoa percentage, dark chocolate can range anywhere from "sweet dark" varieties that contain only 30 percent cocoa products, to semisweet, bittersweet, and finally ultra-dark varieties that border on unsweetened. In this book, whenever I recommend using "dark chocolate," I am referring to a semisweet chocolate with a cocoa percentage around 60 to 65 percent. You can adjust this recommendation, of course, depending on your personal tastes.

Because dark chocolate does not contain milk solids, and milk and white chocolates do, the three types of chocolate behave very differently and should not be interchanged when used as an ingredient in candy recipes. If the chocolate is to be used for dipping candies, however, you can take liberties and dip with whichever chocolate you prefer.

Milk chocolate In addition to containing cocoa solids and cocoa butter, milk chocolate contains either dry milk solids or condensed milk. In the United States, milk chocolate only has to have a cocoa percentage of 10 percent to qualify as chocolate, but this is a pitifully small amount and results in a nearly flavorless candy. I recommend using a milk chocolate with at least 35 percent cocoa solids.

White chocolate White chocolate, with its distinct lack of chocolate flavor and color, has inspired many a debate as to whether it is a true chocolate or not. According to the U.S. Food and Drug Administration (FDA), because white chocolate contains cocoa butter, it can be admitted to the chocolate club. In order to qualify as white chocolate, products must contain at least 20 percent cocoa butter, but I recommend using white chocolates that have at least 30 percent cocoa butter, for the best taste and texture. White chocolate also contains milk solids, flavorings like vanilla, and a good amount of sugar.

Cocoa powder Cocoa powder is an unsweetened powder with a strong chocolate flavor. It comes in two varieties: natural and Dutch-processed (sometimes called "alkalized"). Dutch processing involves treating the cocoa powder to remove sour flavors, and it also gives cocoa powder a deeper chocolate color. Because Dutch processing changes the acidity of the cocoa powder, the two varieties sometimes behave differently depending on the specific recipe. The recipes in this book were tested with Dutch-processed cocoa powder.

Chocolate chips Chocolate chips are great in cookies, but they have no place in most candy recipes. Chips are usually made from low-quality chocolate, meaning they have a weak flavor, and they contain additives that help them hold their shape at higher temperatures. Chocolate chips are extremely thick when melted, and they cannot be used for tempering or coating dipped candies. The one exception to my no-chips-allowed policy is when they are used in recipes to add texture, as in the recipe for Mint Chocolate Chip Truffles on page 95.

Chocolate candy coating Chocolate candy coating is actually a chocolate substitute, used to replace tempered chocolate in dipped confections. You can learn more about candy coating in the How to Temper Chocolate section on page 24.

Dairy Products

Cream Cream and milk are both categorized by the amount of butterfat they contain. Cream varieties include heavy cream, light cream, whipping cream, and manufacturing cream. For the recipes in this book, you should always use heavy cream, which is defined as having between 36 and 40 percent butterfat.

Milk The recipes in this book were developed using whole milk, which contains at least 3.5 percent fat. Whenever possible, select pasteurized milk and cream rather than ultra-pasteurized, which has been heated to an extremely high temperature and lacks a fresh dairy flavor.

Butter Butter is available in salted and unsalted varieties, but I recommend using only unsalted butter. Salt acts as a preservative, meaning that salted butter can sit on store shelves longer and end up tasting less fresh than unsalted butter. Additionally, there are no regulations regarding how much salt is in salted butter, so using unsalted butter gives you a greater degree of control over how much salt your candy actually contains.

Please, don't even think about using margarine in place of butter. It has a higher water content than butter, which can affect the behavior and texture of your candy, and more importantly, the taste is far inferior.

Evaporated milk Evaporated milk is a canned dairy product. As the name suggests, it is made by evaporating much of the water from milk. The advantage of using evaporated milk is that it is shelf-stable, so it is easy to keep a supply on hand in the pantry. Because it has a lower water content, it requires less cooking time when used in candy recipes, making it a convenient ingredient in fudges and caramels.

Sweetened condensed milk Sweetened condensed milk is made by evaporating most of the water from milk and replacing it with a large quantity of sugar. The sugar acts as a preservative, so this canned milk product can be stored even longer than evaporated milk. Sweetened condensed milk is commonly used for making dulce de leche, caramels, and fudges, especially quick microwave fudge recipes.

Flavoring Oils and Extracts

Extracts and oils can add a wonderful punch of flavor to any candy. The most common extract is vanilla, but fruit flavors, mint, and almond are also readily available on any supermarket shelf. Extracts are usually labeled as either natural or imitation. Whenever possible, select all-natural extracts, which have a purer, less chemical taste. When looking to add vanilla flavor, your options are not limited to extract. Vanilla bean paste and the scraped seeds of vanilla beans are both excellent substitutes, and provide a stronger, fresher flavor than vanilla extracts.

Unlike alcohol-based extracts, flavoring oils have the advantage of being able to be mixed directly into melted chocolate without causing it to seize. Additionally, flavoring oils are usually much more potent than extracts, so you can add less and still get a strong, pure flavor. Both oils and extracts should be added to candies at the end of the cooking process, so that the flavoring does not evaporate or boil off.

Salt

Salt enhances the flavor and balances the sweetness of all types of candy. I recommend using kosher salt rather than iodized table salt. Kosher salt has larger grains and less sodium than table salt, and it has less of a harsh chemical flavor. Several recipes in this book call for flaked sea salt to be used as a crunchy garnish. Although these gourmet salts with large, coarse crystals are wonderful for embellishing candies, they should not be used in place of salt in the recipes themselves.

Equipment

Most candies do not require specialty equipment, and if you cook or bake regularly you probably have most of what you need for candy making already in your kitchen. In addition to a few common appliances like a stove, a microwave, and a mixer, here are some tools and accessories that are of particular use in candy making.

Paintbrushes Small paintbrushes can be used to brush a thin layer of chocolate inside of candy molds or candy cups. They are also useful for decorating finished candies with luster dust, gold leaf, or other specialty embellishments. Make sure the brushes you use are clean and have only been used for food handling.

Parchment paper Parchment paper has many uses, including forming paper cones for decorating, covering work surfaces and baking sheets, and providing a smooth, nonstick surface for dipped candies.

Chocolate thermometer To temper chocolate, you will need a digital or glass thermometer that can display temperatures in one-digit increments between the range of 80° and 120°F (26.5° and 50°C).

Candy thermometer Candy thermometers are often labeled "candy/deep-fry thermometers" and have a temperature span from 100° to 400°F

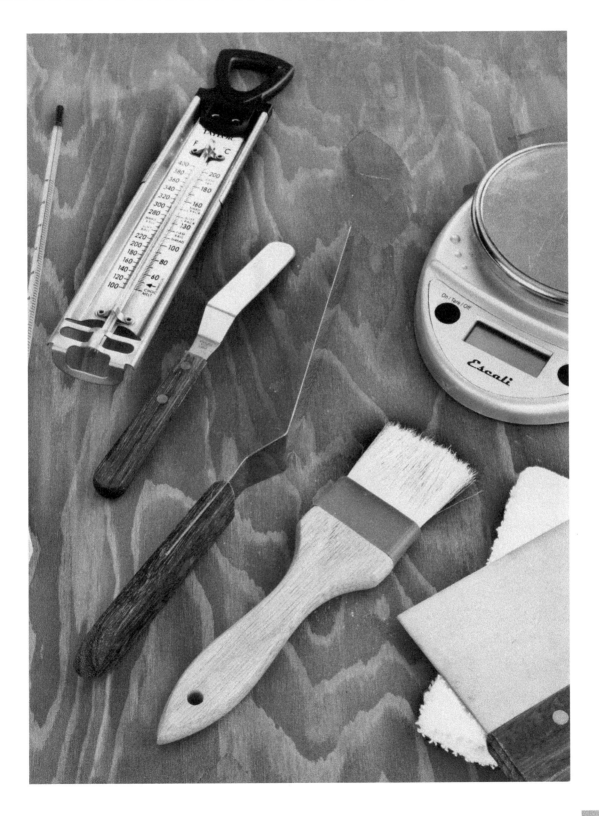

(38° to 204°C). They can range from an inexpensive glass tube to a complex digital thermometer, but make sure whichever thermometer you choose has a clip that allows you to attach it to the side of your saucepan. This leaves your hands free and keeps the bulb from touching the bottom of the pan.

Offset spatulas These metal spatulas with angled blades are my tools of choice for smoothing toffee, fudge, and marshmallows into even layers on baking sheets and in pans. The larger sizes are useful for filling pastry bags and scraping the tops of candy molds, and the smaller sizes are good for finer decorating work.

Pastry brushes Pastry brushes are used to wipe down the sides of the saucepan when cooking sugar candies. Make sure you have a pastry brush that is dedicated for candy work only, so that it does not absorb odors from savory cooking.

Kitchen scale Measuring out your candy ingredients using a kitchen scale is the fastest, most reliable, and most accurate method of measuring. Look for a scale that can display weights in both imperial and metric measurements for the most versatility.

Bench scrapers Bench scrapers can be used to scrape ingredients, clean work surfaces, agitate candies like fondant and fudge, and cut blocks of candy.

Candy scoop A candy scoop is useful when portioning out truffles and other round candies. Scoops are available in a variety of diameters and make the task of creating consistently sized balls of candy fast and efficient.

Pastry bags and tips In candy making, pastry bags are most often used for filling chocolate molds with soft fillings. They can also be used to add decorative touches to candy or for piping candies into special shapes.

Dipping tools While you can easily use a dinner fork for dipping truffles, to get the cleanest results you will want to use dipping tools. They are often sold as a set, with a round or spiral dipper and a forklike dipper with two or three tines. Round dippers are useful for dipping round candies, while fork dippers are good for dipping square truffles, caramels, and other candies with flat bases.

Food coloring and candy coloring In candy making you will use both food coloring and candy coloring. Candy coloring is oil-based, so it mixes well with white chocolate and candy coating. If you try to color chocolate with regular food coloring, which is water-based, the color will appear streaky and the water content might cause the chocolate to seize.

Food coloring can be used for all other types of candy, including hard candies, marshmallows, and ganaches. It comes in liquid, gel, and powdered varieties. I prefer gel coloring, which is more concentrated than the liquid variety and more consistent than the powdered variety. Gel coloring provides strong, deep color while adding a minimal amount of excess moisture, which can skew a candy recipe.

Candy molds There are two main types of candy molds: molds that are intended for chocolate and other low-temperature candies, and molds that are intended for hard candies and other high-temperature uses. Trying to use a chocolate mold to make hard candy can result in a melted mold and a huge mess, so it is important to understand the type of mold you are purchasing and its intended use. Chocolate molds can be either thick polycarbonate or thinner, clear plastic, while hard candy molds can be metal or thick, opaque plastic. See page 29 for additional information about chocolate molds.

Candy cups Candy cups are both an attractive and a practical way to present candy. In addition to making your candies look professional, these miniature foil or paper cups separate them individually, which prevents them from sticking together or becoming scuffed. Candy cups can also be used to mold chocolate cups, as in the recipe for Chocolate Peanut Butter Cups on page 109.

Candy sticks Candy sticks are used to make lollipops. They come in different lengths and widths, so if you are using lollipop molds, be sure to buy the size that corresponds with the openings in your molds.

CHAPTER 2

Candy-Making Techniques

I hope you're ready for candy boot camp, because this chapter is all about mastering fundamental candy techniques. In the following pages, you will learn necessary skills—how to cook sugar, how to temper chocolate, how to mold candy, and how to prepare nuts for cooking. Please read this section carefully, because most success in the kitchen depends on understanding how to properly work with sugar and chocolate.

General Candy-Making Tips

Unfortunately for the sugar fiends among us, candy making can be a time-consuming process. Depending on the recipe, cooking sugar can take anywhere from 15 to 50 minutes, not counting any other recipe preparation steps. The long process can be annoying, but it should not be rushed. To get the best flavor from caramelizing sugar it should be cooked between medium and medium-high heat (the recipe will specify). Do not try to speed the process by turning the heat to the highest setting. This will most likely scorch your candy, leaving you with a sad, burnt-tasting product and a ruined pan.

When selecting a pan for cooking candy, choose pans with a heavy bottom that will distribute heat evenly, and always follow the recipe's recommendations for pan size. Many candies can boil to three or four times their initial size during the cooking process, which can cause messy and frustrating accidents if your pan is too small. If a recipe does not specify an exact quart size, assume that a small pan holds about 1 quart (1 L), a medium pan holds 3 to 4 quarts (2.7 to 3.6 L), and a large pan holds at least 6 quarts (5.4 L).

As a general rule, I do not recommend doubling the recipes in this book. Increasing the recipe quantities sometimes works just fine, but sometimes the extra volume prevents the candy from cooking properly and gives unsatisfactory results.

The measurements in this book are given in both weight and volume. Although it is possible to successfully cook candy using volume measurements, I highly recommend investing in a kitchen scale. Scales can be purchased inexpensively, and they will give you more accurate, consistent results in your cooking. You will also find that recipe preparation goes faster when everything is weighed out, eliminating the need for fumbling with cups and spoons. In addition, there is no reliable way to measure the volume of chopped chocolate, because the weight of 1 cup of chocolate can vary so drastically depending on the type of chocolate and the size of the pieces. As a result, the chocolate measurements in this book are given solely by weight.

Working with Sugar

Working with sugar is not exactly rocket science, but you'll have the best results if you understand just a bit of chemistry. Sugar naturally forms a crystalline state, and the process of cooking sugar involves manipulating these crystals to get a specific outcome and texture in the final candy. For most of the sugar-based candies in this book, granulated sugar is first combined with a liquid to form a sugar syrup.

When making the sugar syrup, you should stir constantly with a plastic spatula, over medium heat, until all of the sugar crystals are completely dissolved. If sugar crystals remain in the syrup, they will encourage other crystals to form, causing your final candy to have a grainy, gritty texture.

If you're using a candy thermometer, don't insert it into the syrup until all of the sugar is dissolved, and the syrup is boiling. This prevents undissolved sugar crystals from clinging to the thermometer and recrystallizing the syrup. Clip the thermometer securely to the side of the pan. To avoid a false reading, make sure the bulb is completely submerged in the syrup and not touching the bottom of the pan.

Sometimes sugar crystals stick to the sides of the pan, so many of the recipes will instruct you to either brush down the sides of the pan with a wet pastry brush to remove any stray crystals or to cover the pan of boiling syrup with a lid, so that the condensation can wash down the sides of the pan and dissolve the crystals.

Finally, there is one more safeguard against crystallization: interfering agents. Don't be dissuaded by the scary name—these substances are actually a huge help to the candy maker. Interfering agents are added to a sugar syrup during cooking to prevent the formation of sugar crystals. The most common agents are acids like lemon juice, vinegar, and cream of tartar, or corn syrup. Adding any of these to your sugar syrup will make the chance of unintentional crystallization less likely, and will allow you to stir the syrup periodically without fear of accidentally introducing sugar crystals into the mixture.

Sugar crystals are not always bad; some candies, like fudge and fondant, depend on the formation of sugar crystals to achieve their characteristic texture. Other candies, however, require a smooth, glasslike finish without a hint of graininess, so take care in your handling of the sugar syrup and follow the instructions on when to stir and when to avoid agitating the boiling sugar.

Calibrating Your Candy Thermometer

Forget fancy copper saucepans, expensive appliances, or gourmet ingredients—an accurate candy thermometer is the most important tool in the candy maker's kitchen. A difference of even a few small degrees in cooking temperature can have a huge impact, so for the best results, make it a regular practice to test the accuracy of your candy thermometer. If you live at a high altitude, testing your thermometer is even more important, because the boiling point of water changes and this can affect sugar cooking temperatures. To test your thermometer, follow these steps:

1. Bring a pot of water to a rolling boil. At sea level, the boiling point of water is 212°F (100°C).

2. Insert your candy thermometer and clip it to the side of the pan. Make sure the bulb is fully submerged in the water but not touching the bottom of the pan. Keep the thermometer in the boiling water for several minutes to ensure an accurate reading.

3. After 2 or 3 minutes, check the temperature. If it reads 212°F (100°C), you know your thermometer is completely accurate! Chances are, however, it might be off by a few degrees, or more, in either direction. Take this temperature difference into account every time you use the thermometer.

Melted sugar can easily crystallize if not handled properly.

For instance, if your thermometer reads 205°F (96°C) in the boiling water, you know that it displays temperatures 7°F (4°C) cooler than they actually are. If a recipe calls for the candy to be cooked to 240°F (115.5°C), you will only need to cook it until your thermometer reads 233°F (111.5°C). If you wait until your thermometer reads 240°F (115.5°C), the candy will actually be quite overcooked! Make a note of the temperature difference so that you can remember your personal "candy thermometer conversion."

Candy thermometers can become less accurate over time, so you should make it a habit to perform this test on a regular basis.

Testing a thermometer in boiling water

Determining Sugar Temperature with the Cold Water Test

Before there were candy thermometers, there was the cold water test to determine the temperature of boiling sugar. Thermometers are now the preferred method for judging candy temperatures accurately, but the cold water method still has its supporters—in fact, I prefer it for testing the finished texture of caramels (see page 59). Here's how to test your candy's temperature without a thermometer:

1. Before you start cooking, place a teaspoon and a small bowl of cold water with a few ice cubes next to the stove.

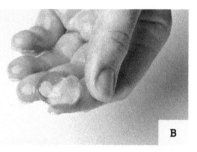

A. THREAD STAGE: The sugar does not hold its shape, but forms thin threads between the fingers (230° to 235°F [110° to 112.8°C]).

B. SOFT BALL STAGE: The sugar can be formed into a ball, but it starts to soften and flatten after a few seconds (235° to 240°F [112.8° to 115.6°C]).

C. FIRM BALL STAGE: The sugar forms a solid ball that can still be compressed between the fingers (245° to 250°F [118.3° to 121°C]).

D. HARD BALL STAGE: The sugar forms a ball that cannot be easily flattened (250° to 265°F [121° to 129.5°C]).

E. SOFT CRACK STAGE: The sugar can be stretched between the fingers to form a piece that will bend slightly before breaking apart (270° to 290°F [132° to 143.3°C]).

F. HARD CRACK STAGE: The sugar immediately forms brittle threads when it is immersed in the ice water and easily breaks into hard pieces (300° to 310°F [149° to 154.5°C]).

G. CARAMEL STAGE: The sugar is fragrant, has an amber color, and is extremely hard and brittle when immersed in water (320° to 350°F [160° to 176.7°C]).

2. Once the sugar syrup is boiling, drop small spoonfuls of it into the ice-cold water.

3. Let it sit for a few seconds, then dip your fingers in, carefully remove the sugar, and check the consistency. The texture of the sugar signals the current temperature of the candy.

Working with Chocolate

The days of the home baker being forced to settle for one or two substandard types of chocolate from the grocery store are long gone. Today there are many excellent brands of fine chocolate readily available to the home consumer, including Valrhona, El Rey, Cacao Barry, Guittard, Lindt, and Callebaut. It's exciting to have so many options, but how do you choose between them?

When selecting chocolate to use in these recipes, let your taste buds be your guide. I have provided several brand recommendations, but don't let those limit you—be adventurous and conduct your own taste test! Choose a chocolate with a flavor and texture you enjoy eating plain. As long as you are following the recipe guidelines and using the recommended dark, milk, or white variety, there is no wrong choice. And if you don't initially find a chocolate to your liking, then taste, taste again.

To store your chocolate, keep it well wrapped in a cool, dry environment, away from strong odors. Chocolate should not be stored in a refrigerator or freezer if possible, because it might absorb condensation that will cause problems when it is later melted or tempered. If your environment is so warm that room temperature is not an option, wrap the chocolate very well in plastic wrap, place it in an airtight container, and store it in the refrigerator. When you remove it from the refrigerator, do not unwrap it until it has come to room temperature. Dark chocolate will keep for over a year, while milk and white chocolate are good for at least six months.

How to Chop Chocolate

If you buy your chocolate in bar form, it should be chopped into small pieces before being melted or tempered. Chocolate is sensitive to overheating, and chopping the chocolate ensures that it melts quickly and evenly, without becoming scorched. Chocolate wafers (known as pistoles) are generally thin enough that they do not need to be chopped.

To chop chocolate you should use either a large chef's knife or a serrated knife with a long blade. To use a chef's knife, begin at one corner of the chocolate bar and angle the blade out at a slight diagonal. Use firm pressure to chop small pieces

A. Chopping chocolate with a chef's knife

B. Chopping chocolate with a serrated knife

off the bar, working your way inward. Periodically rotate the bar and begin at a new corner until the chocolate is chopped into small, even pieces **(A)**.

A serrated knife requires less force than a chef's knife and works well for thinner bars of chocolate. Again beginning at one corner, use a gentle sawing motion to chop off shards of chocolate. Rotate the bar and work your way in from the corners until all of the chocolate is in small pieces that are approximately the same size **(B)**.

How to Melt Chocolate

Melting chocolate seems like a no-brainer, but there are two trouble areas to watch out for in this seemingly simple process: heat and water. If chocolate is overheated, it will become thick, unworkable, and eventually scorched. Water is equally dangerous—even a few drops of water in a bowl of melting chocolate can cause it to "seize," or thicken into a grainy, unappetizing glob. Fortunately, if you are careful, it's easy to avoid these pitfalls.

It is traditional to melt chocolate with a double boiler, but I prefer to use a microwave. It is faster and easier and does not involve boiling water, which always poses a risk of steam or stray water droplets contaminating the chocolate. To melt chocolate in the microwave, place chopped chocolate in a microwave-safe bowl. Melt the chocolate in 30-second intervals, stirring with a rubber spatula after every 30 seconds so that it does not overheat. Stop heating the chocolate when there are still a few chunks remaining, because the residual heat will melt the last bits of chocolate.

If you prefer to use the stovetop, bring 1 inch (2.5 cm) of water to a simmer in the bottom pan of a double boiler. Place the chopped chocolate in the top portion of the double boiler, and set it over the simmering water. Turn the heat off and let the gradual heat of the water melt the chocolate. Stir frequently, and monitor the double boiler to make sure it's not steaming or splattering water into the chocolate. When the chocolate is melted, remove the top of the double boiler and carefully wipe the bottom to remove any condensation.

How to Temper Chocolate

Tempering chocolate is a fundamental skill for the home candy maker, and a necessary step in making many of the chocolate recipes in this book. It has a bad reputation as a difficult, intimidating process, suitable only for professionals, but that couldn't be further from the truth! It is true that tempering, like many culinary skills, does take some practice, but in this section I hope to demystify the process and show how simple tempering can be.

What Is Tempering?

Tempering is the process of heating and cooling melted chocolate to produce gorgeously shiny, professional-looking candies. Simply melting chocolate is not enough to get a flawless chocolate finish, due to the unique chemical makeup of chocolate.

All chocolate contains cocoa butter, a complex fat that has the ability to form different crystalline structures. If chocolate is simply melted without regard to the heating and cooling temperatures, the fat crystals will arrange themselves in a loose, haphazard structure upon cooling. Tempering controls the cooling of the fat crystals and arranges them to form tight, stable bonds.

The question you might now ask is, "So what? Why should I care about the crystalline bonds of my chocolate, as long as it tastes good?" Unfortunately for the science-averse, tempered chocolate has a very different behavior, texture, and even taste when compared to untempered chocolate.

Chocolate that has been tempered is smooth and shiny, with a glossy finish and a slight "snap" when you break it. It sets quickly at cool room temperature, and releases from chocolate molds cleanly and easily. Tempered chocolate has a higher melting point than untempered chocolate, meaning that it does not get soft and sticky at room temperature, is less prone to melting in your hand, and has a pleasant, slow-melting quality in the mouth.

Chocolate that has been melted but not tempered often has a dull, matte look when it sets, and might have white or grayish streaks or spots. This is called "bloom," and it is the result of cocoa butter crystals coming to the surface of the chocolate. Bloom is not harmful, and bloomed chocolate is still completely edible, but the texture is often rough and crumbly, with a muted chocolate flavor. In addition, untempered chocolate is quick to melt at room temperature and become soft when handled, so there are practical as well as aesthetic reasons for using tempered chocolate.

When Should I Temper Chocolate?

Chocolate should be tempered when it is necessary to give your candies a firm texture or a hard, shiny coating. The most common uses for tempered chocolate include dipping truffles and other candies, making molded chocolates, and forming barks and clusters.

There are a few instances when you do not need to worry about tempering chocolate. When chocolate is used as a flavoring ingredient in candy recipes—for instance, when it is melted

into fudge, kneaded into fondant, or incorporated into ganache—it does not need to be tempered. The recipes in this book will always indicate when your chocolate should be tempered.

How Do I Temper Chocolate?

There are many different methods for tempering chocolate, and there is not one definitive "best" way to temper. The process described here, known as the "Seed Method," is the technique I use most frequently, and I think it is the most accessible for beginners. The appeal of this method is that is uses a piece of solid, tempered chocolate to plant "seeds" of good cocoa butter crystals in melted chocolate, greatly accelerating the tempering process.

Before You Begin

Tempering chocolate requires a chocolate thermometer, not to be confused with a candy thermometer. (See page 15 for pictures and descriptions of both thermometers.) A digital thermometer can be used instead, but only if it can provide accurate one-degree readings of temperatures from 80° to 120°F (26.5° to 50°C).

Chocolate tempering works best in a cool, dry environment. It is not impossible to temper chocolate during hot or humid weather, but it is much less predictable. To prevent frustration, try to avoid tempering chocolate on stormy, foggy, or extremely hot days.

Be sure to use real, tempered chocolate. Chocolate chips contain additives that help them keep their shape during baking, and these additives make tempering impossible. Additionally, the chocolate you are using must already be in temper. Examine it carefully to make sure it is hard and shiny, without streaks or spots that indicate

A. Chop three-quarters of the chocolate, and leave one-quarter whole.

B. Melt the chopped chocolate, then add the chocolate chunk.

C. Stir the chunk into the chocolate, letting it melt and release good seed crystals. Monitor the temperature carefully.

D. Once the chocolate has cooled to the prescribed temperature, spread some chocolate on a piece of parchment at room temperature to see whether it sets properly.

E. When the chocolate is tempered, remove the chunk of chocolate.

F. Tempered chocolate on the left, mildly bloomed chocolate in the middle, very bloomed chocolate on the right

bloom. Chocolate is always tempered before it is sold, but if it has been stored or transported in hot weather, it's possible that it has come out of temper. The Seed Method will not work if you use bloomed chocolate.

I recommend beginning with at least 24 ounces (672 g) of chocolate. This may be more than you need for your recipe, but it is difficult to temper small amounts of chocolate, and a large bowl of chocolate will stay in temper longer than a smaller bowl. Any extra chocolate can be saved and remelted for later use, or use it to make some of the barks and clusters in chapter 9 (page 102).

The Tempering Process

Begin by chopping approximately three-quarters of the chocolate into small pieces, as described on page 23. Leave one-quarter of the chocolate unchopped, in one or two large chunks. Place the chopped chocolate in a large microwave-safe bowl, and reserve the chocolate chunk to the side **(A)**.

Microwave the chocolate bowl in 30-second intervals on high heat. Stir the chocolate well with a rubber spatula after every 30 seconds. Periodically insert the chocolate thermometer and take the temperature of the melting chocolate. Heat dark chocolate until it registers 115°F (46°C), and heat white or milk chocolate to 110°F (43.3°C). Do not bring dark chocolate over 120°F (49°C) and milk or white chocolate over 115°F (46°C).

Once your bowl of chocolate is warm enough, add the reserved chunk of chocolate **(B)**. Because the chunk of chocolate is already in temper, as it melts it gradually releases "seeds" of stable cocoa butter crystals that mix with the melted chocolate and encourage it to form a tight, crystalline structure as the chocolate cools. Stir the chocolate frequently—stirring helps the chocolate cool faster, and agitation also aids the tempering process. Be sure to scrape down the bottom and sides of the bowl as you stir.

As you stir the cooling chocolate, you will notice a change in its appearance and texture. When it is warm it is fluid and very shiny, but as it cools and comes into temper, it gets thicker, with more of a glossy, satiny finish. Stir the chocolate until it has cooled to under 90°F (32°C) for dark chocolate, or 87°F (30.6°C) for milk and white chocolate **(C)**.

At this point, smear a spoonful of chocolate onto a piece of parchment paper to test whether it is tempered. If it is in temper, the chocolate will start to set within several minutes, becoming hard and glossy. If you are in a cool room, dark chocolate should set within 4 to 5 minutes, and milk or white chocolate should set within 7 to 8 minutes. Resist the temptation to refrigerate the chocolate and speed the process—this will skew the test results **(D)**.

If the chocolate sets with a firm, shiny finish, congratulations! You have successfully tempered chocolate. Remove the chocolate chunk from the melted chocolate and set it aside. (If it stays in the chocolate, it will continue to lower the temperature of the bowl and your chocolate will quickly become too thick. The chocolate chunk can be saved and reused later.) Your chocolate can now be used in any recipe that calls for tempered chocolate **(E)**.

If the test strip of chocolate does not set, continue to stir the bowl of chocolate and let the temperature drop a few more degrees, then test it again. Different brands of chocolate behave differently, and some require a slightly higher or lower temperature before they come into temper.

HOW CAN I AVOID TEMPERING CHOCOLATE?

Short of hiring a private pastry chef to do all of your chocolate work, you have only two options when it comes to avoiding tempering: keeping your untempered chocolates refrigerated, or using chocolate candy coating. If you decide not to temper, your chocolate candies will need to be stored in, and served directly from, the refrigerator to prevent blooming. This can be a workable solution, but the flavor and texture of your candies might suffer if they are served chilled, and the chocolates will most likely bloom if they are left out at room temperature for an extended period of time.

Candy coating, also known as summer coating or compound coating, is a confectionary product that can be used to replace tempered chocolate for dipping. It should never be used to replace chocolate when it is an ingredient in other recipes, like truffles or fudge. Candy coating is generally sold in wafer form and is available in many different varieties, including dark chocolate, light chocolate, and a rainbow of non-chocolate colors and flavors. The chocolate varieties often contain some amount of cocoa, but they are not true chocolates because they contain other fats, such as palm kernel oil, instead of cocoa butter.

The advantage of candy coating is that it can be melted and used immediately, no tempering required. It's extremely user-friendly, and unlike untempered chocolate, it sets firm and shiny at room temperature. The disadvantage is that the texture and flavor are vastly inferior to those of true chocolate. Candy coating can be a convenient shortcut, especially when time is of the essence or you are dipping only a small number of items, but remember that what you gain in convenience you sacrifice in flavor.

Keeping Chocolate in Temper

Tempering chocolate is only half of the battle—once it is tempered, it needs to be maintained at a working temperature. For dark chocolate this means 86° to 89°F (30° to 31.7°C), and for milk and white chocolate this means 84° to 87°F (29° to 30.6°C). There are several different ways of keeping chocolate in temper. Some cooks like to set the bowl of chocolate on top of a barely warm heating pad wrapped in a towel. Some periodically pass the bowl over a gas burner to warm the bottom. Some microwave the chocolate in short bursts on half power, and some even blast the sides of the bowl with a hair dryer!

Whichever method you choose, make sure the reheated chocolate does not exceed 95°F (35°C) for dark chocolate, or 90°F (32.2°C) for milk or white chocolate. If the chocolate gets above these temperatures, it will go out of temper, and you will need to begin the heating and seeding process again.

And Remember…

Although there is a fair amount of science behind the tempering of chocolate, it is also an art, and success requires practice. The good news is that unless it has scorched or seized, chocolate is forgiving. If you make mistakes and do not temper it correctly, you can simply remelt it and start again. This is all part of the delicious process of chocolate experimentation!

How to Use Chocolate Molds

Chocolate molds can be used to form intricately shaped chocolates that are impossible to create by hand. Inexpensive molds are made of thin plastic and are widely available at many craft stores. They work well but are more prone to breaking or cracking after periods of heavy use. Professional-grade molds are more expensive but will last longer. They are usually made of heavy polycarbonate and can be found at specialty candy and kitchen supply stores, as well as through online retailers. (See the Resources section on page 140.)

Although chocolate molds can be used to create solid chocolate candies, they are more often used to make chocolates with soft centers, such as buttercream, nut paste, caramel, or ganache. When selecting a mold for filled chocolates, keep in mind that the cavities need to be deep enough to contain the outer chocolate shell as well as a generous amount of filling. Shallow molds are best saved for solid chocolate candies.

The most important rule of using chocolate molds is that you should always use tempered chocolate. Tempered chocolate contracts upon cooling, so it releases easily from chocolate molds. Using chocolate that is melted but not tempered is a recipe for frustration, because the chocolate might not release cleanly or have a finished shine.

To make molded chocolates, spoon tempered chocolate into the cavities of a chocolate mold. Tap the mold gently against the countertop to remove any air bubbles from the chocolate **(A)**. Let the chocolate sit at room temperature for several minutes, so that the chocolate thickens and just starts to set around the edges. Then, turn the mold upside down over the chocolate bowl or a piece of parchment paper and let the excess

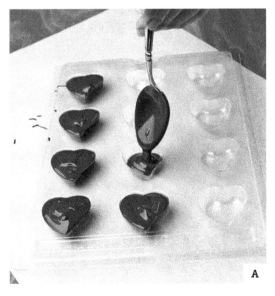

A. Spoon tempered chocolate into the cavities.

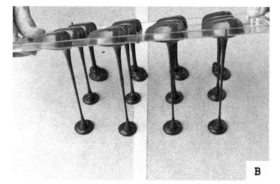

B

F

C

G

D

B. Once the chocolate starts to set, invert the mold and let excess chocolate drip out.

C. Scrape excess chocolate from the top of the mold.

D. Pipe or spoon the filling into the cavities, leaving space at the top to seal them with chocolate.

E. Cover each cavity with tempered chocolate.

F. Scrape the top of the mold again to level the backs of the candies and remove excess chocolate.

G. Once completely set, gently flex the mold to loosen the chocolates, then invert the mold to release them.

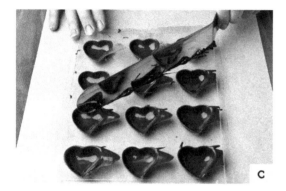

E

chocolate drip out of the mold **(B)**. Use a large chef's knife, a bench scraper, or the side of an offset spatula to scrape the top of the mold clean and remove any excess chocolate. This step will help produce clean edges on your molded chocolates **(C)**. See images on page 30.

Let the chocolate set completely in the molds before filling the cavities. Pipe or spoon the filling into the cavities, making sure you leave room at the top for another layer of chocolate. In some cases, like with caramels, it is easiest to fill the molds if the filling is fluid and slightly warm. Make sure the temperature of the filling does not exceed 80°F (26.5°C)—any warmer and you risk taking the chocolate out of temper **(D)**.

Refrigerate the mold to set the filling, if it is fluid. Once set, spoon additional tempered chocolate on top of the filling **(E)**. Scrape across the top of the mold again to remove excess chocolate from the top of the candies **(F)**. Let the chocolate set completely at room temperature, for about 20 minutes. Once set, refrigerate the molds for an additional 20 minutes—this will cause the chocolate to constrict and make it easy to remove the candies.

When you are ready to unmold your chocolates, gently bend the mold to loosen the chocolates. Invert the mold over a sheet of parchment and flex it so that the chocolates drop out of the cavities **(G)**.

Working with Nuts

Nuts are a natural addition to many confections. They have a slightly sweet, slightly savory flavor and a pleasing crunch that makes them the perfect match for chocolate and sugar candies. Despite their charms, they can still be lackluster if improperly prepared—there are few things more disappointing than soft, pale, flavorless nuts! In this section you will learn how to toast, skin, and chop your nuts to get the best flavor and texture in your candy recipes.

How to Toast Nuts

When it comes to toasting nuts, slow and steady wins the race. You will get better, more consistent results if you toast them at a lower temperature for a longer period of time than if you try to rush things by cranking up the oven. Unless a specific recipe notes otherwise, begin by preheating the oven to 325°F (162°C, or gas mark 3). Spread the nuts in a single layer on a baking sheet. I recommend using a shiny aluminum sheet as opposed to a double-insulated or dark black baking sheet, because the aluminum sheet will transmit heat evenly without burning the bottom of the nuts.

Bake the nuts for 10 to 15 minutes, depending on the size and number of nuts. Stir them with a spatula every 3 to 4 minutes to prevent those around the edges from burning. Your nuts are done when their color has deepened on both sides and they are noticeably fragrant. Let them cool at room temperature and then check the texture to make sure they are as toasted and crisp as you want them. If not, return them to the oven for a few more minutes.

A

B

C

D

How to Skin Nuts

Some nuts, like hazelnuts and almonds, are often sold with their thin, papery skins still on the nuts. Although these skins are not harmful, many people find the texture distracting and the taste bitter, so it is best to remove them before cooking with them.

To skin hazelnuts, toast them on a baking sheet for about 10 minutes at 325°F (162°C, or gas mark 3) **(A)**. The hazelnuts are ready when they are fragrant and brown and their outer skins have split apart **(B)**. Remove the nuts from the oven and let them cool for a few minutes. When they are warm but no longer hot, take a rough kitchen towel in your hands and place a handful of hazelnuts in the middle **(C)**. Close up the top of the towel and vigorously rub the hazelnuts between your hands, using the friction of the towel against the nuts to peel off the skin. Repeat this process until you have removed the skins from all of your hazelnuts **(D)**. Some nuts are particularly stubborn, so don't be discouraged if they're not pristine—a small amount of skin remaining on the nuts is normal.

To skin almonds, they need to be blanched instead of toasted. Bring a pot of water to a boil and drop the almonds into the boiling water **(A)**. Cook them for 1 minute, then drain the nuts and

A. Toast hazelnuts for about 10 minutes at 325°F (162°C, or gas mark 3).

B. The hazelnuts are ready when their outer skins have split apart, as shown.

C. Put a handful of nuts in a kitchen towel and rub vigorously.

D. Repeat until you have removed the skin from all the nuts.

let them cool. Once the nuts are cool enough to handle, pinch them between your fingers so that the nuts slide out of the outer skin **(B)**. After they have been skinned, they can be toasted like any other nut **(C)**.

How to Chop Nuts

Many recipes call for nuts that are either "coarsely chopped," "finely chopped," or "ground." For the first two instances I prefer to chop nuts by hand, rather than using a tool like a food processor. To chop nuts, gather them in a circle on your cutting board and use a large, sharp chef's knife. Keep the tip of the blade down and let the heavy handle do the work. As you lift and lower the handle, rotate the knife around the circle to reach all the nuts. They will shift and roll, so periodically gather them back together into a clump. Continue chopping until the nuts are the size required for the recipe.

If the recipe calls for ground nuts, use a food processor to obtain the best results. Place the nuts in the processor and pulse it in short bursts, checking the nuts frequently. Stop mixing when the nuts are finely ground but are still individual pieces. Because of the high oil content, it's easy to overprocess nuts and end up with oily clumps or nut butter. Similarly, never chop or grind nuts when they are warm, because the oils are more volatile and you are liable to have greasy nuts as a result.

A. Cook raw almonds for 1 minute in boiling water, then drain.

B. Once they have cooled, pinch them so the nuts slide out of the skin.

C. After they are skinned they are ready to be used or toasted.

PART II

Candy Recipes

CHAPTER 3

Sugar Candies

Sugar is the indisputable foundation of candy making. It gives flavor and body to all types of candies, and is a versatile chameleon in the kitchen. Just by mixing it with a few other ingredients and cooking it to various temperatures, you can produce soft chewy caramels, creamy fudges, or light and crispy toffees. While sugar pairs well with dairy, chocolate, fruit, nuts, and just about anything else, it's equally delicious when prepared simply, with minimal additions and adornments. This chapter celebrates sugar candy in its most basic form, and these recipes for lollipops, fruit chews, taffy, and more will make you a believer in the simple power of sugar.

Troubleshooting Sugar Candies

My hard candies are soft or sticky.

If your hard candies stick to your teeth, stick to one another, or are otherwise too soft, it means they have too much moisture. One likely culprit is high humidity. Humidity is the enemy of sugar work, and whenever possible, you should avoid cooking sugar candies during humid or stormy weather. Sugar is hygroscopic, meaning it absorbs water easily, and if your kitchen is too humid, the candy will absorb that excess moisture. Possible outcomes of cooking sugar in humid weather include the candy taking longer to cook, becoming unpleasantly sticky, or failing to set up altogether. Even if your weather is not humid, regular kitchen activities, like running the dishwasher or having a pot of boiling water on the stove, can greatly increase the humidity in your kitchen.

Another possible reason for sticky candies is that the hard candy was not cooked to a high enough temperature. Before making another batch of candy, calibrate your thermometer as described on page 20, and make sure you cook future batches to the temperature specified in the recipe.

Finally, hard candies will eventually become sticky even in a low-humidity environment if left unwrapped, so after the candies are formed they should be well wrapped and kept in an airtight container for long-term storage.

My hard candies taste like burned sugar.

Hard candy should be cooked to approximately 300°F (149°C), or the hard-crack stage (see page 22). At this temperature, the candies will become brittle and hard, but the sugar has not yet caramelized. If the candies are cooked to a higher temperature, the sugar will take on a darker color and flavor and, eventually, burn. If your candy has the taste of burned sugar, it has been cooked to too high a temperature. Calibrate your thermometer as described on page 20 and cook it to the proper, lower, temperature in the future.

My hard candies are gritty or grainy.

If your hard candies are coarse or gritty instead of smooth, this means that the sugar has started to crystallize. Sugar crystals might have been introduced by over-vigorous stirring, not washing down the sides of the pan properly, or stirring with a spoon that has undissolved sugar on it. The best way to prevent grainy candy is to be very conscientious about how you stir and cook sugar syrups in the future.

Lollipops

YIELD: 8 LARGE (2-INCH, OR 5-CM) LOLLIPOPS

4 ounces or ½ cup (120 ml) water

7 ounces or 1 cup (196 g) granulated sugar

11 ounces or 1 cup (308 g) light corn syrup

1 to 2 teaspoons flavoring extract (see Note below)

3 or 4 drops gel food coloring of your choice

Prepare your hard candy lollipop molds by coating the cavities with a very light layer of nonstick cooking spray or vegetable oil. Insert lollipop sticks into the molds and set aside for now.

Combine the water, granulated sugar, and corn syrup in a 2-quart (1.8-L) saucepan over medium-high heat. Stir until the sugar dissolves, then wash down the sides of the pan with a wet pastry brush to prevent sugar crystals from forming. When the sugar syrup comes to a boil, insert a candy thermometer.

Continue to cook the sugar syrup, stirring occasionally, until the thermometer reads 300°F (149°C). Remove the pan from the heat, and let the candy stop bubbling completely. Once it is still, stir in the flavoring extract and the food coloring of your choice.

Carefully spoon the hot sugar syrup into the prepared molds, making sure that the tops of the sticks are covered with syrup and are well embedded in the candy. Let the lollipops sit and harden at room temperature until they are completely cool and firm. Once cool, don't pull them out by the sticks. Instead, carefully flex the back of the molds to remove the lollipops without causing any breakage.

Lollipops keep well when stored in a cool, dry environment. For best results, wrap them individually in plastic wrap and store them in an airtight container at room temperature for up to a month.

—

VARIATION: To make sour lollipops, add 1 teaspoon of citric acid to the sugar syrup when you add the flavoring and color. Citric acid adds a tart, tangy flavor. For ideas on where to find citric acid, see the Resources section on page 140.

NOTE

The strength of extracts varies greatly from brand to brand and flavor to flavor. Some, like vanilla, are quite mild, while others, like peppermint and cinnamon, are very strong. It may take some trial and error to determine how much flavoring to add to suit your taste. Never add the flavoring until the candy stops bubbling; if you add it too early, the heat from the candy will just cook off most of the flavor. If you are using flavoring oils, they are much stronger than extracts, so start by adding just ¼ to ½ teaspoon flavoring oil.

Caramel by the Sea Lollipops

YIELD: 8 LARGE (2-INCH, OR 5-CM) LOLLIPOPS

1 ounce or 2 tablespoons (28 ml) water

2¾ ounces or ¼ cup (77 g) light corn syrup

1 teaspoon lemon juice

7 ounces or 1 cup (196 g) granulated sugar

1 teaspoon sea salt

2 ounces or 4 tablespoons (56 g) unsalted butter, cubed

1 teaspoon vanilla extract

Flaked sea salt, for finishing (optional)

Prepare your hard candy lollipop molds by coating the cavities with a very light layer of nonstick cooking spray or vegetable oil. Insert lollipop sticks into the molds and set aside for now.

In a 2-quart (1.8-L) saucepan, combine the water, light corn syrup, lemon juice, granulated sugar, and sea salt. Place the pan over medium-high heat, and stir until the sugar dissolves. Wash down the sides of the pan with a wet pastry brush to prevent sugar crystals from forming.

When the sugar syrup comes to a boil, insert a candy thermometer, then gradually add the cubes of butter one at a time and stir them in. Continue to cook the candy, stirring occasionally, until the thermometer reads 300°F (149°C). Remove the pan from the heat and stir in the vanilla extract.

Carefully spoon the hot sugar syrup into the prepared molds, making sure that the tops of the sticks are covered with syrup and are well embedded in the candy. Let the lollipops sit and harden at room temperature until they are completely cool and firm. Once cool, don't pull them out by the sticks. Instead, carefully flex the back of the molds to remove the lollipops without causing any breakage. If desired, sprinkle the tops with a pinch of flaked sea salt.

Lollipops keep well when stored in a cool, dry environment. For best results, wrap them individually in plastic wrap and store them in an airtight container at room temperature for up to a month.

Lemon Meringue Lollipops

YIELD: 8 LARGE (2-INCH, OR 5-CM) LOLLIPOPS

FOR LEMON LAYER

2 ounces or ¼ cup (56 ml) water

3½ ounces or ½ cup (98 g) granulated sugar

5½ ounces or ½ cup (154 g) light corn syrup

1 teaspoon lemon extract

¾ teaspoon citric acid (see Note below)

2 or 3 drops yellow gel food coloring

FOR MERINGUE LAYER

2 ounces or ¼ cup (56 ml) water

3½ ounces or ½ cup (98 g) granulated sugar

5½ ounces or ½ cup (154 g) light corn syrup

1 teaspoon marshmallow flavoring (see Note below)

1 teaspoon no-color vanilla extract (see Note below)

½ teaspoon white food coloring

This recipe works best with lollipop molds that are at least ¼ inch (6 mm) deep. Prepare your molds by coating the cavities with a very light layer of nonstick cooking spray or vegetable oil.

To make the lemon layer: In a small saucepan, combine the water, granulated sugar, and light corn syrup. Stir until the sugar dissolves, then wash down the sides of the pan with a wet pastry brush to prevent sugar crystals from forming. When the sugar syrup comes to a boil, insert a candy thermometer.

Continue to cook the sugar syrup, stirring occasionally, until the thermometer reads 300°F (149°C). Remove the pan from the heat, and let the candy stop bubbling completely. Once it is still, stir in the lemon extract, citric acid, and yellow food coloring.

Carefully spoon the hot sugar syrup into the prepared molds, filling each cavity approximately halfway. Insert the lollipop sticks into the cavities. Let the lemon layer cool while you wash the pan and thermometer and prepare the meringue layer.

To make the meringue layer: Make the meringue layer the same way you made the lemon layer, cooking and stirring the water, granulated sugar, and light corn syrup in a saucepan. Once the candy reaches 300°F (149°C), remove the pan from the heat, allow the bubbles to stop, then add the marshmallow flavoring, no-color vanilla extract, and white food coloring.

Spoon the syrup on top of the lemon layer, coming all the way to the top of the mold. Let the lollipops sit and harden at room temperature until they are completely cool and firm. Once cool, don't pull them out by the sticks. Instead, carefully flex the back of the molds to remove the lollipops without causing any breakage.

Lollipops keep well when stored in a cool, dry environment. For best results, wrap them individually in plastic wrap and store them in an airtight container at room temperature for up to a month.

Broken Glass

YIELD: 1 POUND 2 OUNCES (504 G)

4 ounces or ½ cup (120 ml) water

8¼ ounces or ¾ cup (231 g) light corn syrup

14 ounces or 2 cups (392 g) granulated sugar

2 to 4 teaspoons flavoring extract (see Note below)

½ teaspoon gel food coloring

½ cup (60 g) powdered sugar

Line a baking sheet with a nonstick silicone mat or a layer of aluminum foil sprayed with nonstick cooking spray.

In a medium saucepan, combine the water, corn syrup, and granulated sugar. Stir until the sugar dissolves, then wash down the sides of the pan with a wet pastry brush to prevent sugar crystals from forming. When the sugar syrup comes to a boil, insert a candy thermometer.

Continue to cook the sugar syrup, stirring occasionally, until the thermometer reads 300°F (149°C). Remove the pan from the heat, and let the candy stop bubbling completely. Once it is still, stir in the flavoring extract and food coloring. If you want to make two different colors and flavors of broken glass candy from one batch, pour half of the sugar syrup into a separate pan before you add the extract and food coloring. Work quickly and add different colors and flavors to the two batches, so that the candy does not start to set in the pans.

Pour the candy out onto the prepared baking sheet and let it spread into a thin layer. Cool the candy completely at room temperature. Once it is set, pull it up from the sheet and crack it into small pieces by banging it against a cutting board or shattering it with a knife handle.

Place the powdered sugar in a zip-top plastic bag and add the shards of candy. Shake the bag until the candy is coated with the powdered sugar. Store the candy in an airtight container at room temperature. If kept well wrapped in a low-humidity environment, this candy can last for several months.

NOTE

The strength of extracts varies greatly from brand to brand and flavor to flavor. It may take a little trial and error to determine how much flavoring to add to suit your taste. If you are using flavoring oils, they are much stronger than extracts, so start by adding just ½ teaspoon flavoring oil.

Butterscotch Buttons

2⅔ ounces or ⅓ cup (75 ml) water

2⅔ ounces or ⅓ cup (75 ml) heavy cream

7 ounces or 1 cup (196 g) granulated sugar

¼ teaspoon salt

⅛ teaspoon cream of tartar

1½ ounces or 3 tablespoons (42 g) unsalted butter, at room temperature

½ teaspoon vanilla extract

You can either use silicone molds to make these candies or make free-form circles by hand. If you are going to pour them into circles, cover two baking sheets with silicone mats or aluminum foil sprayed with nonstick cooking spray.

In a 2-quart (1.8-L) saucepan, combine the water, heavy cream, granulated sugar, salt, and cream of tartar over medium-high heat. Stir until the sugar dissolves, then wash down the sides of the pan with a wet pastry brush to prevent sugar crystals from forming. When the sugar syrup comes to a boil, insert a candy thermometer.

When the candy reaches 240°F (115°C), add the butter and stir it in. Continue to cook the candy, stirring occasionally, until it reaches 280°F (138°C). At this point, remove the pan from the heat and stir in the vanilla extract.

If you are using silicone molds, quickly spoon the butterscotch into the cavities and let the candy set completely. Once set, pop out the Butterscotch Buttons. If you are pouring the candy into circles, use a small spoon to drop spoonfuls of the hot syrup onto the prepared baking sheets. Work quickly, before the candy starts to set, and leave a little space in between each drop because they will spread. Allow the drops to set completely, then gently lift them from the baking sheet.

Store Butterscotch Buttons in an airtight container at room temperature for up to 2 weeks.

Fruit Chews

2 ounces or 4 tablespoons
(56 g) unsalted butter

5½ ounces or ½ cup (154 g)
light corn syrup

5¼ ounces or ¾ cup (161 g)
granulated sugar

1 teaspoon fruit-flavored
extract

½ teaspoon citric acid
(see Note below)

1 or 2 drops gel food coloring

Line a 9 x 5-inch (23 x 12.7-cm) loaf pan with aluminum foil and spray the foil with nonstick cooking spray.

In a medium saucepan, combine the butter, corn syrup, and granulated sugar. Place the saucepan over medium-high heat, and stir until the butter melts and the sugar dissolves. Wash down the sides of the pan with a wet pastry brush to prevent sugar crystals from forming. When the sugar syrup comes to a boil, insert a candy thermometer.

Continue to boil the candy, stirring occasionally, until the thermometer reads 245°F (118°C). This temperature will produce a candy that is soft enough to chew but holds its shape fairly well. For softer candies, cook the syrup to 242°F (116.7°C), and for firmer candies, cook it to 248°F (120°C).

Once at the proper temperature, remove the pan from the heat and stir in the extract, citric acid, and food coloring. Pour the candy into the prepared pan. Let it set at room temperature until it is completely cool and firm.

Once firm, remove the candy from the pan and peel off the foil backing. Use a large sharp knife to cut it into small 1 x 1-inch (2.5 x 2.5-cm) squares. Wrap the squares in waxed paper so they don't stick together or lose their shape. Store Fruit Chews in an airtight container at room temperature for up to a month.

NOTE

Citric acid is an optional ingredient, but it adds a tanginess that makes the fruit flavors more realistic. For ideas on where to find citric acid, see the Resources section on page 140.

Saltwater Taffy

YIELD: 2 POUNDS (908 G), OR ABOUT 100 (1-INCH, OR 2.5-CM) PIECES

4 ounces or ½ cup (120 ml) water

11 ounces or 1 cup (308 g) light corn syrup

14 ounces or 2 cups (392 g) granulated sugar

¾ teaspoon salt

1 ounce or 2 tablespoons (28 g) unsalted butter

1 teaspoon flavoring extract

1 ounce or ¼ cup (28 g) marshmallow creme

3 or 4 drops gel food coloring

Spray a rimmed baking sheet with nonstick cooking spray.

Combine the water, corn syrup, granulated sugar, and salt in a 4-quart (3.6-L) saucepan over medium-high heat. Stir until the sugar dissolves, then wash down the sides of the pan with a wet pastry brush to prevent sugar crystals from forming. When the sugar syrup comes to a boil, insert a candy thermometer.

Cook the syrup, without stirring, until the thermometer reaches 255°F (124°C). This temperature will produce a wonderfully soft and chewy taffy. If you like your taffy stiffer, cook it to 260°F (126.7°C) for a medium-firm taffy or 265°F (129.5°C) for a very firm taffy. Once at the proper temperature, remove the pan from the heat, add the butter and flavoring, and stir until the butter melts and everything is well mixed.

(continued on next page)

Pour the candy onto the prepared baking sheet and let it spread out. Add the marshmallow creme and food coloring on top. Let the candy cool until it starts to set around the edges, about 5 to 10 minutes. Slide a spatula under one edge of the candy and fold it into the center, over the marshmallow creme, then fold the other edges of the candy into the middle, making a compact package.

Put on food-safe plastic gloves to protect your hands, and spray your gloves with nonstick spray. Gather up the candy and knead it together in your hands until the marshmallow creme and coloring are mixed in. Holding the candy in both hands, pull your hands apart, stretching the candy into a rope between them. Bring your hands back together, twist the candy together, and repeat the pulling process. At first the taffy will droop and fall, but as you continue to pull the taffy, it will cool down and become firmer and easier to manipulate.

Continue to pull the taffy for 20 minutes, until it holds its shape well and becomes difficult to pull. You will start to see parallel ridges in the pulled candy toward the end of the process—this is a sign the taffy is ready.

Divide the taffy into quarters to make it easier to work with. Roll the taffy into a long thin rope about ½ inch (1.3 cm) in diameter. Use oiled kitchen shears or a sharp knife to cut it into small 1-inch (2.5-cm) pieces, and repeat with the remaining taffy. Wrap the taffy in waxed paper to help it keep its shape and prevent it from sticking together.

Store Saltwater Taffy in an airtight container at room temperature for up to 2 weeks. You can keep it longer, but over time it will start to lose its soft and chewy texture.

—

VARIATION: To make striped taffy, prepare two baking sheets, and divide the sugar syrup evenly between them. Add half of the marshmallow creme to each batch, and add different colors on top. Pull each batch individually, and roll them into long thin ropes. Twist the ropes of different colored taffy together, then pull them thin so that the colors blend. Cut and wrap the striped taffy as usual.

HOW TO MAKE SALTWATER TAFFY

A. Combine the water, corn syrup, sugar, and salt in a medium saucepan.

B. Bring the sugar syrup to a boil and cook it to 255°F (124°C).

C. Remove the pan from the heat and stir in the butter and flavoring extract.

D. Pour the candy onto a baking sheet sprayed with nonstick cooking spray.

E. Add the marshmallow creme and food coloring on top of the candy and let it cool until the edges start to set.

F. Slide a spatula under the edge of the candy and fold it into the center.

G. Bring all of the candy together into a packet.

H. Knead the candy together with your hands until the marshmallow creme and coloring are mixed in. Begin to pull the candy apart between your hands.

I. At first the candy will be soft and will droop, but continue to pull it for 20 minutes.

J. By the end, the candy will hold its shape and will show parallel ridges when you pull it between your hands.

K. Roll the taffy into thin ropes and cut it into small 1-inch (2.5-cm) pieces.

L. Wrap the individual pieces of taffy in waxed paper.

CHAPTER 4

Fondant

These days, fondant might be best known as the thick sugar paste used to cover wedding cakes and specialty desserts. But don't confuse that fondant—known as "rolled fondant"—with traditional candy fondant. Candy fondant is a versatile sugar-based dough that can be used to make everything from soft cream centers to the liquid filling in chocolate-covered cherries. In its simplest state, fondant is a simple mix of sugar, corn syrup, and water—not much different than a basic lollipop recipe! But whereas the goal with lollipops and other sugar candy is to avoid crystallization, making fondant depends on the formation of crystals through a precise heating, cooling, and stirring process. You will be amazed to see how your thin, clear fondant syrup can be transformed into a thick, opaque candy dough just by the act of stirring.

Troubleshooting Fondant

My fondant is unpleasantly grainy.

After it is boiled, fondant needs to cool to a specific temperature before it can be stirred. If the fondant is agitated before it has cooled properly, large sugar crystals might form, resulting in a grainy texture to the finished fondant.

My fondant is too soft.

Soft fondant can be caused by several factors. If it is humid, the fondant can be absorbing the moisture from the air, resulting in a soft and sticky candy. It is also possible that the sugar syrup was not cooked to a high enough temperature. Make sure your thermometer is calibrated following the directions on page 20, and carefully cook the sugar syrup to the prescribed temperature. Finally, it could be that the fondant was not agitated enough during the stirring stage. There is no risk of overworking fondant, so if you are not sure whether the fondant is done, continue to stir a little longer. For a quick fix, try kneading in small amounts of powdered sugar until it is firm enough to work with.

My fondant is old and hard to knead.

If you have old fondant that is too stiff to knead by hand, microwave it in 5-second bursts, turning it after every 5 seconds so that it heats evenly. Try to knead it after every microwave session, and stop heating it once you are able to knead it by hand. Soften the fondant by kneading it like bread dough until it is smooth and supple.

Old-Fashioned Fondant

YIELD: 2 POUNDS (908 G)

4 ounces or ½ cup (120 ml) water

5½ ounces or ½ cup (154 g) light corn syrup

1 pound 12 ounces or 4 cups (784 g) granulated sugar

Powdered sugar, for dusting

In a 4-quart (3.6-L) saucepan, combine the water, corn syrup, and granulated sugar. Stir until the sugar dissolves, then wash down the sides of the pan with a wet pastry brush to prevent sugar crystals from forming. When the sugar syrup comes to a boil, insert a candy thermometer.

Cook the syrup, without stirring, until the thermometer reaches 238°F (114°C). Pour the syrup into a 9 x 13-inch (23 x 33-cm) pan, but do not scrape down the sides and bottom of the saucepan. Insert the candy thermometer, and let the syrup cool, undisturbed, until it reaches 120°F (49°C).

Once at 120°F (50°C), use a stiff plastic or wooden spoon to start stirring the fondant in a figure-eight pattern. Swirl the spoon through the candy, then gather it all together in the center of the pan and repeat. During this process, the clear, sticky syrup will gradually become more creamy and opaque.

(continued on next page)

HOW TO MAKE OLD-FASHIONED FONDANT

A. Combine the water, corn syrup, and sugar in a 4-quart (3.6-L) saucepan over medium-high heat, and bring it to a boil.

B. Brush down the sides of the pan with a wet pastry brush.

C. Cook the sugar syrup to 238°F (114°C).

D. Pour the syrup into a 9 x 13-inch (23 x 33-cm) pan and let it cool to 120°F (50°C).

E. Begin to stir the syrup in a figure-eight pattern with a stiff spoon.

F. The syrup will start to lose its shine and become white and creamy.

G. As you stir, the candy will become thicker and more opaque.

H. Finally, the fondant will be so stiff it will be difficult to stir.

I. Knead the fondant like bread dough until it becomes smooth.

J. When the fondant is shiny and pliable, wrap it well and let it sit overnight.

TO COLOR AND FLAVOR FONDANT

K. Form the fondant into a disc and add the desired colors and flavorings. Fold the fondant over on itself.

L. Knead the fondant on a work surface dusted with powdered sugar.

M. Continue kneading until the color and flavoring are completely incorporated.

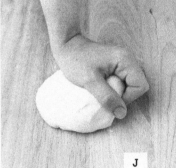

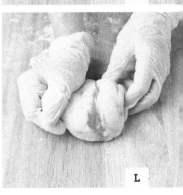

Continue to stir the fondant as it becomes thicker, until eventually it is stiff and difficult to stir. It might even become so stiff that it starts to crumble. Once you can no longer stir it, wet your hands and gather the fondant into a ball. Dust a work surface with powdered sugar and knead the fondant like bread dough until the texture has smoothed out, any crumbliness is gone, and it is supple and pliable.

If you want to add flavoring or coloring to the fondant (see Variations, below), shape it into a disc and add the flavoring or coloring to the center. Fold the fondant over on itself and knead until the flavoring or color is well dispersed, dusting your hands and the fondant with powdered sugar as necessary to prevent it from getting too sticky. Wrap the fondant well in plastic wrap and for the best texture, allow it to sit overnight before using it.

Old-Fashioned Fondant can be stored in an airtight container at room temperature for up to a month.

—

VARIATIONS: To make chocolate fondant, melt 4 ounces (112 g) dark chocolate and let it cool to room temperature. Add the melted chocolate to 1 pound (454 g) fondant and knead them together by hand or mix them together in a mixer until the chocolate is completely incorporated.

To make coconut fondant, add 1½ teaspoons coconut extract to 1 pound (454 g) fondant and knead it in. Roll the fondant into small balls, and roll the balls in shredded sweetened coconut.

To make nutty fondant, knead together 5 ounces or ½ cup (140 g) praline paste or nut butter and 1 pound (454 g) fondant. Roll the fondant into small balls, and roll the balls in crushed nuts.

To make s'mores fondant, knead 1¼ ounces or ½ cup (35 g) miniature marshmallows into chocolate fondant. Roll the fondant into small balls, and roll the balls in coarsely crushed graham crackers.

NOTE

You can also make fondant with a mixer instead of stirring by hand. To use a mixer, pour the cooked sugar syrup into a mixing bowl and cool it to 120°F (50°C). Once cooled, mix the fondant on medium speed until it is thick, white, and opaque, about 10 to 12 minutes. If necessary, knead it by hand to smooth it out at the end.

Peanut Butter and Jelly Fondant Sandwiches

YIELD: 36 CANDIES

1 pound (454 g) Old-Fashioned Fondant (page 50)

Powdered sugar, for dusting

3¼ ounces or ⅓ cup (91 g) smooth peanut butter

⅛ teaspoon salt

¼ teaspoon raspberry flavoring

⅛ teaspoon citric acid (see Note below)

Red and purple gel food coloring

12 ounces (336 g) peanut butter–flavored candy coating

Chopped freeze-dried berries or chopped peanuts, for decorating (optional)

NOTE

Citric acid adds a tart, tangy flavor to the raspberry fondant. For ideas on where to find citric acid, see the Resources section on page 140.

Divide the fondant into two 8-ounce (227-g) portions. Dust your hands and a work surface with powdered sugar, and knead together one 8-ounce (227-g) portion of fondant with the peanut butter and salt. Knead until the fondant is smooth and the peanut butter is completely mixed in. Wrap the peanut butter fondant in plastic wrap and set it aside for a moment.

Add the raspberry flavoring, the citric acid, and a few drops of red and purple food coloring to the other 8-ounce (227-g) portion of fondant and knead everything together.

Place the raspberry fondant between two sheets of parchment or waxed paper and roll out into a thin rectangle 6 inches (15 cm) wide by 12 inches (30.5 cm) long. Roll the peanut butter fondant until it is also a 6 x 12-inch (15 x 30.5-cm) rectangle and refrigerate both fondant rectangles until firm.

Once firm, carefully place the raspberry fondant on top of the peanut butter fondant and gently roll over them with a rolling pin to press them together. Cut the fondant rectangle in half, so that you have two squares 6 inches (15 cm) across. Trim any uneven edges so that your squares are neat and tidy. Stack one square on top of the other, so you are left with one 6 x 6-inch (15 x 15-cm) square comprised of 4 alternating layers of peanut butter and raspberry fondant. Cut the fondant into 36 small 1-inch (2.5-cm) squares. If it is too soft to cut cleanly, refrigerate it briefly until it can be neatly cut.

Melt the peanut butter–flavored candy coating in the microwave. Dip each fondant sandwich into the melted coating, and place the dipped pieces on a piece of parchment or waxed paper. If desired, sprinkle the tops with chopped freeze-dried berries or peanuts while the coating is still wet. Let the coating set completely at room temperature before serving.

Store Peanut Butter and Jelly Fondant Sandwiches in an airtight container at room temperature for up to 2 weeks.

Soft Buttercreams

12 ounces (336 g) chocolate of your choice, melted and tempered (see page 24)

6 ounces (168 g) freshly made Old-Fashioned Fondant (page 50)

1 to 2 ounces (28 to 56 g) unsalted butter, at room temperature

Food coloring of your choice

Flavoring extracts of your choice

Line twenty-four 1-inch (2.5-cm) chocolate molds with tempered chocolate, following the instructions on page 29. Make sure the chocolate lining the molds is completely set.

Mix the fondant and 1 ounce (28 g) softened butter in a mixer until it is smooth and soft. If the fondant you are using is very stiff, or if you enjoy a stronger butter flavor, add the remaining 1 ounce (28 g) butter to get your ideal taste and texture. If you would like to make different flavors of buttercream from one batch, divide the buttercream into different bowls and add a small amount of food coloring and flavoring extract, to taste, to each bowl.

Pipe or spoon the buttercream mixture into the prepared molds, being sure to leave room at the top to seal the molds with chocolate. Once the molds are filled, refrigerate the molds for 20 minutes until the buttercream mixture is firm.

Seal the tops of the molds with tempered chocolate and let the chocolate set for 20 minutes at room temperature, then refrigerate them for 10 minutes more. Once set, carefully remove the chocolates from the molds and let them come to room temperature before serving.

Store Soft Buttercreams in an airtight container in the refrigerator for up to 2 weeks, but for the best taste and texture, serve them at room temperature.

Melting Mint Patties

YIELD: 72 CANDIES

Powdered sugar, for dusting

1 pound (454 g) freshly made Old-Fashioned Fondant (page 50)

¾ teaspoon peppermint extract

½ teaspoon invertase (see sidebar, page 56)

1 pound (454 g) dark chocolate, melted and tempered (see page 24)

Dust your work surface and your hands with powdered sugar, and knead together the fondant, peppermint extract, and invertase. Alternately, you can chop the fondant into pieces and mix the fondant, extract, and invertase together on low speed in a mixer using the paddle attachment.

Roll the fondant into small balls about ½ inch (1.3 cm) wide and place them on a parchment-lined baking sheet. You should get about 6 dozen small balls from the fondant. Gently press down on top of each ball so that it is a disc almost ¾ inch (2 cm) wide. Refrigerate the discs until completely firm.

(continued on next page)

Once firm, dip the mint patties into the tempered chocolate and let them set at room temperature. Check the patties, and if any of them have areas on the sides or bottom that are not covered with chocolate, dip them again. Because the centers get so soft, the filling will leak out of any undipped areas. When the chocolate is completely set, store the mint patties in an airtight container at room temperature for 4 to 5 days to give the centers time to soften and liquefy.

After they have softened, Melting Mint Patties can be stored in an airtight container at room temperature for up to 2 weeks.

WHAT IS INVERTASE?

Invertase is a naturally occurring enzyme that, when added to sugar-based candies, gradually breaks down the sugar molecules and causes the candy's texture to soften. It's most commonly available as a clear liquid.

The amount of invertase needed depends upon the recipe and the desired final texture, but in general it only takes a small amount of invertase to soften firm candies—between ¼ and ½ teaspoon invertase per pound (454 g) of fondant is a good guideline. It usually takes anywhere from 4 to 10 days for the invertase to work, so be prepared to make your candies in advance. Candies made with invertase should be kept at room temperature because cold temperatures can slow the enzyme's reaction.

Chocolate-Covered Cherries

YIELD: 30 CANDIES

1 (10-ounce, or 280-g) jar maraschino cherries with stems (to yield about 30 cherries)

1 pound (454 g) freshly made Old-Fashioned Fondant (page 50)

½ teaspoon invertase (see sidebar, page 56)

½ teaspoon almond extract

Pink food coloring (optional)

1 pound (454 g) dark chocolate, melted and tempered (see page 24)

Drain the cherries but reserve the liquid. Spread the cherries in a single layer on paper towels and carefully pat them dry.

Fill the bottom pan of a double boiler with water, and bring it to a simmer. Place the fondant in the top pan of the double boiler and place it over the simmering water. Heat the fondant, stirring frequently, until it is liquid. Add a candy thermometer and continue to heat the fondant until it reaches 160°F (71°C).

Remove the pan from the heat and stir in the invertase, almond extract, and pink food coloring, if desired. Hold a cherry by the stem and dip it until it is submerged in the fondant. Pull it out of the fondant, letting the excess drip back into the pan. Set the cherry down on a parchment-covered baking sheet and make sure the stem is pointing straight up.

Repeat until all of the cherries are dipped. If the fondant starts to get too thick, place it back over the water bath to warm it, and add a spoonful or two of reserved cherry juice as necessary to thin it into a dippable consistency.

Let the cherries sit at room temperature for 10 minutes, until the fondant is completely set and hard.

Dip the fondant-covered cherries into the tempered chocolate, making sure the chocolate completely covers the fondant up to the top of the stem. If any part of the cherry remains uncovered, the liquefying fondant will leak out, so it's important to dip the cherries carefully and thoroughly. Let the chocolate set at room temperature, then store the cherries in an airtight container for a week to give the fondant time to liquefy. Once liquid, Chocolate-Covered Cherries can be stored for an additional 2 weeks at room temperature.

CHAPTER 5

Caramels

The best caramels perform a delicate balancing act. They hold their shape and have a chewy "pull" when you bite into them, but they quickly soften and dissolve in your mouth. They have the deep flavor of long-boiled sugar, cooked until fragrant and caramelized, but the sweetness is tempered by the rich taste of cooked butter and cream. The contradictions between these competing flavors and textures are what make caramels such a complex, delicious candy. The recipes in this chapter highlight the best of what caramels have to offer by pairing them with spices, nuts, fruit, flowers, chocolate, and more.

Troubleshooting Caramels

My caramels are too soft.

Caramels that are too soft have not been cooked to a high enough temperature. Make sure that your candy thermometer is calibrated, as described on page 20, and be very mindful of the temperature when cooking your next batch of caramels. Even a difference of two or three degrees can have a powerful effect on the texture of the finished caramel.

In most instances, it is possible to recook your caramels to try and make them firmer. Scrape the soft caramel into a large saucepan and add ½ cup (120 ml) of water. Stir the mixture over low heat until the caramel melts, then increase the heat and insert a candy thermometer. Cook the caramel until it reaches the prescribed temperature. Add flavoring extracts, because the extended boiling time will have cooked off the original flavoring. The recooked caramels will be a darker color, because the dairy has had more time to caramelize. If you don't want to recook, you can melt them with additional cream to make a delicious caramel dessert sauce.

My caramels are too hard.

Again, the problem of caramel texture comes down to the final cooking temperature. If the caramels are too hard, they have been cooked to too high a temperature. You can attempt to recook them using the method described above. If you don't want to recook them, consider chopping them up into small pieces and using them as caramel chips for baking.

How can I get my caramels just right?

Although nothing can beat the accuracy of a well-calibrated candy thermometer, I think that the cold water test, described on page 21, is the best way of achieving the perfect caramel texture. The problem comes down to personal preference: one person's ideal caramel may be considered "too firm" or "too soft" by someone else. You can bypass this problem entirely by checking the texture of the caramel as it cooks. Once the cooking caramel reaches 240°F (115.5°C), begin performing the cold water test periodically by dipping a spoonful of cooked caramel into a bowl of very cold water. After a few moments, taste the caramel, and when it reaches the texture you desire, remove your caramels from the heat. If you are adding butter after the caramels have cooked, keep in mind that this will soften the caramels a bit, so cook them a little firmer than you would otherwise.

HOW TO MAKE CARAMELS

Every caramel recipe is a little different, but here is a general guide to making traditional caramels.

A. Combine the cream and butter in a small saucepan and bring to a simmer over medium-low heat. Remove the pan from the heat and cover it to keep the dairy warm.

B. In a separate saucepan, combine the corn syrup and sugar over medium-high heat and stir until the sugar dissolves. Cover the pan and bring the mixture to a boil. Boil, covered, for 4 minutes, then remove the lid.

C. Insert a candy thermometer and cook without stirring until the temperature is 320°F (160°C).

D. Pour the warm cream into the hot sugar syrup and stir.

E. Continue to cook, stirring occasionally, as the mixture becomes darker and more fragrant. Cook the caramel to 250°F (121°C) for soft caramels, or 255°F (124°C) for firm caramels.

F. Remove the pan from the heat and add the remaining butter and additional flavorings as desired.

G. Pour the caramel into the prepared pan and let it set at room temperature until firm.

H. Use a large sharp knife to cut the caramel into small pieces. Wrap the caramel squares individually in waxed paper.

Autumn Caramels

YIELD: 1 POUND 14 OUNCES (840 G)

1 vanilla bean

2 cinnamon sticks, broken in half

6 whole cloves, coarsely crushed

1 whole allspice, coarsely crushed

12 ounces or 1½ cups (336 ml) heavy cream

4 ounces or 8 tablespoons (112 g) unsalted butter, divided

11 ounces or 1 cup (308 g) light corn syrup

14 ounces or 2 cups (392 g) granulated sugar

1 teaspoon salt

1 teaspoon vanilla extract

Line an 8 x 8-inch (20 x 20-cm) pan with aluminum foil and spray the foil with nonstick cooking spray.

Split the vanilla bean lengthwise and scrape out the seeds. In a small saucepan, place the vanilla bean seeds, the scraped vanilla pod, the cinnamon sticks, the crushed cloves, the crushed allspice, the heavy cream, and 2 ounces (56 g) of the butter. Place the pan over medium heat and bring the mixture to a low boil. Remove the pan from the heat, cover it with a tight-fitting lid, and let it sit for 30 minutes to infuse the flavors.

After 30 minutes, combine the corn syrup and the granulated sugar in a 4-quart (3.6-L) saucepan and place the pan over medium-high heat. Stir until the sugar dissolves and the mixture comes to a boil. Cover the pan with a lid and let it boil for 4 minutes, so the condensation will wash the sugar crystals from the sides of the pan.

Remove the lid and insert a candy thermometer. Continue to cook the sugar, without stirring, until it reaches 320°F (160°C) on the candy thermometer. Once at 320°F (160°C), carefully pour the warm cream through a strainer into the hot sugar syrup, straining out the vanilla pod, cinnamon sticks, cloves, and allspice. The mixture will bubble and splatter a great deal, and the temperature will drop.

Cook the caramel, stirring frequently, until it reaches 250°F (121°C). This will give you a soft, chewy caramel. If you prefer firmer caramels, cook the candy to 255°F (124°C).

Remove the pan from the heat and stir in the remaining 2 ounces (56 g) butter, the salt, and the vanilla extract, then pour the caramel into the prepared pan. Let it set at room temperature until firm, at least 4 hours or overnight. Once set, remove the candy from the pan and peel off the foil from the back. Use a large sharp knife to cut the caramels into small squares. Wrap each individual caramel in waxed paper to prevent them from sticking together or losing their shape. Store Autumn Caramels in an airtight container at room temperature for up to 2 weeks.

Mango-Macadamia Nut Caramels

YIELD: 1 POUND 4 OUNCES (560 G)

5 ounces or 1 cup (140 g) toasted, salted macadamia nuts, coarsely chopped (see page 33)

1 pound 2 ounces or 2 cups (504 g) mango juice, strained

7 ounces or 1 cup (196 g) granulated sugar

7½ ounces or 1 cup (210 g) packed brown sugar

1 tablespoon (15 ml) fresh lemon juice

4 ounces (112 g) unsalted butter

2⅔ ounces or ⅓ cup (80 ml) heavy cream

½ teaspoon salt

1 teaspoon vanilla extract

Line an 8 x 8-inch (20 x 20-cm) pan with aluminum foil and spray the foil with nonstick cooking spray. Scatter the macadamia nuts over the bottom of the pan.

Pour the mango juice into a 4-quart (3.6-L) saucepan and place the pan over medium heat. Bring the juice to a boil and cook it, stirring frequently to prevent scorching, until it reduces down to ⅓ cup (80 ml) of liquid. Depending on your stove, this will take 30 to 40 minutes.

Remove the pan from the heat and stir in both sugars, the lemon juice, the butter, the cream, and the salt. Return the pan to medium-high heat and stir until the sugar dissolves, then bring the mixture to a boil. Wash down the sides of the pan with a wet pastry brush to prevent sugar crystals from forming. Insert a candy thermometer and cook the caramel, stirring occasionally, until the thermometer reads 245°F (118°C). This produces a caramel with a medium-firm texture. For a stiffer caramel, cook it to 248°F (120°C), and for a softer caramel, cook it to 242°F (116.7°C).

Take the pan off the heat and stir in the vanilla. Pour the caramel over the nuts in the pan and let it set at room temperature until firm, about 4 hours or overnight. Once set, remove the candy from the pan and peel off the foil from the back. Use a large sharp knife to cut the caramels into small squares. Wrap each individual caramel in waxed paper to prevent them from sticking together or losing their shape. Store Mango–Macadamia Nut Caramels in an airtight container at room temperature for up to 2 weeks.

Lavender Caramels

8 ounces or 1 cup (235 ml) heavy cream

2½ ounces or 5 tablespoons (70 g) unsalted butter

1 tablespoon dried lavender

2 ounces or ¼ cup (60 ml) water

2¾ ounces or ¼ cup (77 g) light corn syrup

10½ ounces or 1½ cups (294 g) granulated sugar

1 teaspoon salt

Line an 8 x 8-inch (20 x 20-cm) pan with aluminum foil and spray the foil with nonstick cooking spray.

In a small saucepan, combine the cream, butter, and lavender. Place the pan over medium heat and bring the mixture to a low boil. Remove the pan from the heat, cover it with a tight-fitting lid, and let it sit for 20 minutes to infuse the flavors.

After 20 minutes, combine the water, corn syrup, sugar, and salt in a 4-quart (3.6-L) saucepan and place the pan over medium-high heat. Stir until the sugar dissolves and the mixture comes to a boil. Cover the pan with a lid and let it boil for 4 minutes, so the condensation will wash the sugar crystals from the sides of the pan.

Remove the lid and insert a candy thermometer. Continue to cook the sugar, without stirring, until it reaches 320°F (160°C) on the candy thermometer. Once at 320°F (160°C), carefully pour the warm cream through a wire-mesh strainer into the hot sugar syrup, straining out the lavender. The mixture will bubble and splatter a great deal, and the temperature will drop.

Cook the caramel, stirring frequently, until it reaches 250°F (121°C). This will give you a soft, chewy caramel. If you prefer firmer caramels, cook the candy to 255°F (124°C). Remove the pan from the heat and pour the caramel into the prepared pan.

Let the caramel set at room temperature until firm, at least 4 hours or overnight. Once set, remove the candy from the pan and peel off the foil from the back. Use a large sharp knife to cut the caramels into small squares. Wrap each individual caramel in waxed paper to prevent them from sticking together or losing their shape. Store Lavender Caramels in an airtight container at room temperature for up to 2 weeks.

Pecan Pie Caramels

YIELD: 1½ POUNDS (681 G)

8 ounces or 1 cup (235 ml) heavy cream

3 ounces or 6 tablespoons (84 g) unsalted butter

¾ teaspoon salt

3½ ounces or ½ cup (98 g) granulated sugar

3¾ ounces or ½ cup (105 g) packed brown sugar

5½ ounces or ½ cup (154 g) pure maple syrup

2¾ ounces or ¼ cup (77 g) light corn syrup

2 ounces or ¼ cup (60 ml) water

1½ teaspoons cinnamon

3½ ounces or 1 cup (98 g) toasted pecans, coarsely chopped (see page 33)

Line an 8 x 8-inch (20 x 20-cm) pan with aluminum foil and spray the foil with nonstick cooking spray.

In a small saucepan, combine the cream, butter, and salt. Place the pan over medium heat and bring the mixture to a low boil. Remove the pan from the heat and cover it with a lid to keep warm.

In a 4-quart (3.6-L) saucepan, combine both sugars, the maple syrup, the corn syrup, and the water. Place the pan over medium-high heat, stir until the sugars dissolve, and bring the mixture to a boil. Wash down the sides of the pan with a wet pastry brush to prevent crystallization.

Insert a candy thermometer and continue to cook the sugar, without stirring, until it reaches 240°F (115°C). Once it reaches this temperature, add the warm cream and carefully stir it in. The mixture will bubble and splatter a great deal, and the temperature will drop.

Cook the caramel, stirring frequently, until it reaches 245°F (118°C). This will give you a soft, chewy caramel. If you prefer firmer caramels, cook the candy to 248°F (120°C). Remove the pan from the heat and stir in the cinnamon and the pecans. Pour the caramel into the prepared pan.

Let the caramel set at room temperature until firm, at least 4 hours or overnight. Once set, remove the candy from the pan and peel off the foil from the back. Use a large sharp knife to cut the caramels into small pieces. Wrap each individual caramel in waxed paper to prevent them from sticking together or losing their shape. Store Pecan Pie Caramels in an airtight container at room temperature for up to 2 weeks.

Sea Salt Caramels

YIELD: 2 POUNDS 10 OUNCES (1176 G)

1 pound or 2 cups (470 ml) heavy cream

5½ ounces or ½ cup (154 g) sweetened condensed milk

1 teaspoon sea salt

4 ounces or ½ cup (120 ml) water

1 pound 6 ounces or 2 cups (616 g) light corn syrup

14 ounces or 2 cups (392 g) granulated sugar

4 ounces or ½ cup (112 g) unsalted butter, cubed, at room temperature

Flaked sea salt, for finishing

Line a 9 x 9-inch (23 x 23-cm) pan with aluminum foil and spray the foil with nonstick cooking spray.

In a small saucepan, combine the cream, sweetened condensed milk, and salt. Place the pan over medium heat and bring the mixture to a low boil. Remove the pan from the heat and cover it with a lid to keep warm.

In a 4-quart (3.6-L) saucepan, combine the water, light corn syrup, and granulated sugar. Place the pan over medium-high heat, stir until the sugar dissolves, and bring the mixture to a boil. Wash down the sides of the pan with a wet pastry brush to prevent crystallization.

Insert a candy thermometer and continue to cook the sugar, without stirring, until it reaches 250°F (121°C). Once it reaches this temperature, add the cubed butter and the warm cream and carefully stir everything together. The mixture will bubble and splatter a great deal, and the temperature will drop.

Cook the caramel, stirring frequently to avoid scorching, until it reaches 245°F (118.3°C) and is a golden brown color, about 30 minutes. Pour the caramel into the prepared pan, but don't scrape the bottom and sides of the pan.

Let the caramel set at room temperature until firm, at least 4 hours or overnight. Once set, remove the candy from the pan and peel off the foil from the back. Use a large sharp knife to cut the caramels into small pieces. Sprinkle the top of each piece with a pinch of flaked sea salt. Wrap each individual caramel in waxed paper to prevent them from sticking together or losing their shape. Store Sea Salt Caramels in an airtight container at room temperature for up to 2 weeks.

Caramel Crunch Candy Bars

YIELD: 8 CANDY BARS, APPROXIMATELY 2¾ OUNCES (77 G) EACH

8 ounces (224 g) soft caramels

2 ounces or about 2 cups (54 g) crispy rice cereal

12 ounces (336 g) dark chocolate, melted and tempered (see page 24)

Line an 8 x 4-inch (20 x 10-cm) loaf pan with foil and spray with nonstick cooking spray.

If you are using caramels that are individually wrapped, unwrap them and place them in a microwave-safe bowl. Heat them in 30-second intervals until melted, then pour into the prepared pan. Refrigerate the caramel block until it has set, about 45 minutes.

Cut the caramels widthwise into 8 strips, approximately 1 inch (2.5 cm) wide and 4 inches (10 cm) long. If necessary, refrigerate the caramel strips on a parchment-covered baking sheet until they are very firm.

Place the crispy rice cereal in a wide, shallow bowl. Once the caramel strips are firm, dip one strip in the tempered chocolate, and let the excess drip back into the chocolate bowl. Roll the dipped caramel in the cereal until it is completely coated, then place it back on the baking sheet. Repeat until all of the caramel strips are covered with crispy rice cereal, then refrigerate the candy bars for 30 minutes to set the chocolate.

Dip the candy bars in chocolate a second time, to cover the cereal layer, then let the chocolate set completely. Store Caramel Crunch Candy Bars in an airtight container in the refrigerator for up to a month, and let them come to room temperature before serving.

CHAPTER 6

Toffee

Although the process of making toffee involves cooking a sugar syrup to high heat, just like many hard candy recipes, toffee has one thing most lollipops and hard candies don't have: butter. Gobs and gobs of beautiful, creamy butter. Although the high butter content can make cooking toffee a little tricky, it's more than worth the extra effort to be rewarded with rich, crunchy toffee, bursting with the toasty, caramelized flavors of cooked butter and sugar. These toffee recipes run the gamut from the ultra-traditional English Toffee to more adventurous flavors like Spicy Peanut Butter Toffee with chipotle chili powder.

Troubleshooting Toffee

The butter separated out of my toffee.

Many toffee recipes contain a large amount of butter, and in the course of cooking the candy, it is not uncommon for the butter to separate from the rest of the toffee and appear as a slick, oily layer on top of the bubbling sugar.

There are several common causes of butter separation. If the candy is heated too quickly, the abrupt temperature shift can cause the butter to separate, so it is best to follow the recipe's temperature guidelines and heat the toffee gradually, especially in the beginning stages of melting the butter and the sugar. Another frequent culprit? Thin saucepans that don't conduct heat evenly and have "hot spots" where portions of the candy overheat.

When toffee separates, a layer of butter appears on top of the candy.

If your toffee does separate during cooking, all is not lost. Briefly remove the pan from the heat and stir vigorously to bring the candy back together. If it doesn't come together, return the pan to the heat and add a spoonful of very hot water and stir until the butter is reincorporated. If you don't notice the separation until after the toffee has been poured out of the pan, it is unfortunately too late to fix the toffee, but it's still quite edible! Once it has set, wipe the butter off the top of the toffee and give it a try. If you find the texture a little hard, you can chop up the toffee to use as toffee bits in baking recipes.

My toffee is soft and sticky.

Soft, sticky toffee is caused by an excess of moisture in the candy. This can be a result of undercooking the candy, using a recipe with too much corn syrup or other liquid sweeteners, or making toffee on a humid day. Soft toffee cannot be saved, but in the future you can avoid the problem by making sure your thermometer is calibrated (see page 20), cooking the toffee to the prescribed temperature, and cooking toffee in a low-humidity environment.

English Toffee

YIELD: 1 POUND (454 G) PLAIN TOFFEE, OR 2 POUNDS (908 G) CHOCOLATE-COATED TOFFEE; APPROXIMATELY TWENTY-FOUR 1 X 2-INCH (2.5 X 5-CM) TOFFEE BARS, EACH ABOUT 1 OUNCE (28 G) WHEN COATED IN CHOCOLATE

2⅔ ounces or ⅓ cup (80 ml) water

1½ ounces or 2 tablespoons (42 g) light corn syrup

1 pound or 2 cups (454 g) unsalted butter, at room temperature

1 pound 2⅔ ounces or 2⅔ cups (522.5 g) granulated sugar

1 teaspoon salt

1 pound (454 g) dark chocolate, melted and tempered (optional, see page 24)

Line a rimmed baking sheet with a nonstick silicone mat or aluminum foil sprayed with nonstick cooking spray.

In a 4-quart (3.6-L) saucepan, combine the water, corn syrup, butter, granulated sugar, and salt. Place the pan over medium heat, and stir while the butter melts and the sugar dissolves. Brush down the sides of the pan with a wet pastry brush to prevent sugar crystals from forming, and bring the candy to a boil. Once boiling, insert a candy thermometer.

Continue to cook the candy, stirring frequently to prevent scorching, until it reaches 300°F (149°C).

Once at 300°F (149°C), pour the candy out onto the prepared baking sheet and spread it into a thin layer. Let it set for a few minutes, and then when it is no longer liquid but still pliable, use a knife or a pizza cutter to score the toffee into small 1 x 2-inch (2.5 x 5-cm) rectangles. Let the toffee cool completely at room temperature.

When the toffee is cool, carefully break it apart along the scored lines. You can serve it plain, or you can dip it partially or completely in melted, tempered chocolate. If you dip it in chocolate, you can decorate the top by touching the top with the tines of a dipping fork (see page 127) to give it a nice pattern. This toffee also pairs well with nuts, so consider sprinkling the toffee with your favorite toasted nuts to add a little more flavor and crunch.

Store English Toffee in an airtight container at cool room temperature for up to 2 weeks. In humid environments it might start to get soft and sticky within a week.

Hazelnut Toffee

YIELD: 1 POUND (454 G)

8 ounces or 1 cup (224 g) unsalted butter, cubed

1 ounce or 2 tablespoons (28 ml) water

¾ ounce or 1 tablespoon (21 g) light corn syrup

7 ounces or 1 cup (196 g) granulated sugar

1 teaspoon ground cinnamon

4 ounces or ¾ cup (112 g) toasted hazelnuts, coarsely chopped (see page 33)

Line a rimmed baking sheet with a nonstick silicone mat or aluminum foil sprayed with nonstick cooking spray.

Place the cubed butter in a medium saucepan over medium heat, and gently warm it until it is mostly melted. Once it is almost completely liquid, add the water, corn syrup, and granulated sugar. Stir until the sugar dissolves, then brush down the sides of the pan with a wet pastry brush. Bring the candy to a boil, and insert a candy thermometer. Continue to cook the candy, stirring occasionally to prevent scorching, until it reaches 295°F (146°C) on the thermometer.

Once at 295°F (146°C), remove the pan from the heat and stir in the ground cinnamon until it is well incorporated. Add the hazelnuts, mix them in well, and scrape the toffee onto the prepared baking sheet. Smooth it into a thin, even layer and let it set at room temperature, for about an hour.

When the toffee is set, break or cut it into small pieces to serve. Store Hazelnut Toffee in an airtight container at cool room temperature for up to 2 weeks. In humid environments it might start to get soft and sticky within a week.

Almond Toffee

YIELD: 1 POUND 10 OUNCES (728 G)

12½ ounces or 2½ cups (350 g) whole almonds, raw

8 ounces or 1 cup (224 g) unsalted butter, cubed

4 ounces or ½ cup (120 ml) warm water

7 ounces or 1 cup (196 g) granulated sugar

1 teaspoon salt

1 teaspoon light corn syrup

8 ounces (224 g) dark chocolate, finely chopped

Preheat the oven to 350°F (176.7°C, or gas mark 4). Line a rimmed baking sheet with a nonstick silicone mat or aluminum foil. Spread the almonds on the baking sheet and toast for about 10 minutes, until they are fragrant and light golden brown. Let the almonds cool to room temperature, then take 1 cup (150 g) of toasted almonds and finely chop them by hand or in a food processor. (See page 33 for more information on toasting and chopping nuts.)

Line a rimmed baking sheet with a nonstick silicone mat or aluminum foil sprayed with nonstick cooking spray.

Place the cubed butter in a medium saucepan over medium heat, and gently warm it until it is mostly melted. Once it is almost completely liquid, add the water, granulated sugar, salt, and corn syrup. Stir until the sugar dissolves, then brush down the sides of the pan with a wet pastry brush. Bring the candy to a boil, and insert a candy thermometer. Continue to cook the candy, stirring occasionally, until it reaches 240°F (115°C) on the thermometer.

Add the remaining 1½ cups (200 g) of whole almonds to the toffee, and stir them in. The mixture might separate when you add the nuts, but continue to stir and heat the toffee gently, and it will come back together. Cook the candy, stirring constantly, until it reaches 295°F (146°C) on the candy thermometer. As it gets closer to the temperature the nuts will become fragrant and might start popping, and the toffee will be a deep golden brown color.

Pour the candy out onto the prepared baking sheet and smooth it into an even layer. Let it cool slightly at room temperature, for about 5 minutes, then sprinkle half of the chopped chocolate on top. Allow the chocolate to soften and melt from the heat of the toffee, then spread the melted chocolate into a thin, even layer. Sprinkle half of the crushed nuts on the wet chocolate and press down gently to adhere them.

Refrigerate the tray to set the chocolate, for about 20 minutes. Once set, flip the toffee over and peel off the foil backing. Melt the remaining chopped chocolate in the microwave, spread the melted

chocolate on the toffee, and sprinkle the top with the remaining chopped nuts. Refrigerate the toffee again to set the chocolate, for about 20 minutes. Once set, break or chop the toffee into small pieces.

Store Almond Toffee in an airtight container at cool room temperature for up to 2 weeks. In humid environments it might start to get soft and sticky within a week.

Spicy Peanut Butter Toffee

YIELD: 1 POUND 10 OUNCES (728 G)

2⅔ ounces or ⅓ cup (80 ml) water

3⅔ ounces or ⅓ cup (102 g) light corn syrup

7 ounces or 1 cup (196 g) granulated sugar

9¾ ounces or 1 cup (273 g) crunchy peanut butter

⅛ teaspoon baking soda

¼ teaspoon chipotle chile powder

4¾ ounces or 1 cup (133 g) honey-roasted peanuts, coarsely chopped

6 ounces (168 g) milk chocolate, melted and tempered (see page 24)

Line a rimmed baking sheet with a nonstick silicone mat or aluminum foil sprayed with nonstick cooking spray.

In a medium saucepan, combine the water, corn syrup, and granulated sugar over medium-high heat. Stir until the sugar dissolves, then wipe down the sides of the pan with a wet pastry brush to prevent sugar crystals from forming. Bring the mixture to a boil, and insert a candy thermometer.

Cook the candy, stirring occasionally, until it reaches 305°F (152°C) on the thermometer. Once at the right temperature, remove the pan from the heat and stir in the peanut butter, baking soda, and chile powder. The baking soda will cause the mixture to bubble up and become very foamy. Once it bubbles up, add the chopped peanuts and stir them in as well.

Scrape the toffee onto the prepared baking sheet and smooth it into a thin, even layer. Let the toffee set at room temperature, for about 45 minutes. Once set, spread the top of the toffee with the tempered milk chocolate and allow the chocolate to set. Break or chop the toffee into small pieces to serve it.

Wrap Spicy Peanut Butter Toffee in plastic wrap and store it in an airtight container at room temperature for up to 2 weeks.

—

VARIATION: If you want to turn this toffee into a crispy peanut butter candy bar, pour the toffee into a 9 x 9-inch (23 x 23-cm) pan lined with foil to produce a thicker filling. While it is still warm, run a knife through it to score it into small bars. Once cool, carefully cut the bars along the scored lines and dip them in tempered chocolate.

Cashew Toffee Bars

YIELD: APPROXIMATELY 27 SMALL (1 X 3-INCH, OR 2.5 X 7.5-CM) BARS

8 ounces (224 g) unsalted butter, cubed

11¼ ounces or 1½ cups (315 g) packed light brown sugar

1 tablespoon light corn syrup

½ teaspoon salt

15 ounces or 3 cups (420 g) toasted, salted cashews, coarsely chopped (see page 33)

12 ounces (336 g) dark chocolate, melted and tempered (see page 24)

Line a 9 x 9-inch (23 x 23-cm) pan with aluminum foil and spray the foil with nonstick cooking spray.

Place the cubed butter in a medium saucepan over medium heat, and gently warm it until it is mostly melted. Once it is almost completely liquid, add the brown sugar, corn syrup, and salt. Stir until the sugar dissolves, then brush down the sides of the pan with a wet pastry brush. The butter may separate out at first, but continue stirring and it will come together.

Bring the candy to a boil, and insert a candy thermometer. Continue to cook the candy, stirring frequently to prevent scorching, until it reaches 295°F (146°C) on the thermometer.

Once at 295°F (146°C), remove the pan from the heat and stir in 1 cup (140 g) of the chopped cashews. Pour the toffee into the prepared pan. Let it cool for about 5 minutes, then when it is still pliable but no longer liquid, use a knife to score it into small bars about 1 inch (2.5 cm) wide and 3 inches (7.5 cm) long.

Let the toffee set completely at room temperature. While you wait for it to set, finely chop the remaining 2 cups (280 g) of cashews and place them in a wide, shallow bowl. Once the toffee is cool and firm, carefully cut it along the scored lines and trim any jagged edges.

Dip a toffee bar in the melted chocolate, then roll it in the crushed nuts until it is completely coated on all sides. Repeat until all of the toffee bars have been covered in chocolate and nuts. Refrigerate the bars to set the chocolate, about 15 minutes.

Store Cashew Toffee Bars in an airtight container in the refrigerator for up to 3 weeks, and bring them to room temperature before serving.

CHAPTER 7

Fudge

Traditional fudge, or what I term "old-fashioned fudge," is actually a close relative of fondant. It shares the same cooking process and theory: a sugar syrup is boiled, then cooled to a specific temperature, then beaten just until it starts to crystallize. When done properly, this type of fudge has a texture that cannot be imitated; firm creamy, and smooth, it's an absolute pleasure to taste. But old-fashioned fudge isn't the only game in town. "No-fail" fudge recipes have become more popular. These shortcut fudges use chocolate and marshmallows to help the fudge set and give it a smooth texture, eliminating the need for long periods of cooling and beating.

Troubleshooting Fudge

My old-fashioned fudge is grainy.

A gritty texture is one of the most common complaints when making old-fashioned fudge. Unfortunately, fudge has a tendency to develop sugar crystals extremely easily. Always pay close attention to the recipe, and avoid stirring or agitating the fudge whenever you are not explicitly instructed to do so. It is especially important to let the fudge rest, undisturbed, during the cooling process, and to let it cool all the way to the specified temperature before stirring. Stirring the fudge when it should be cooling, or even vigorously jostling the pan, is a recipe for crystallization. And that's one candy recipe no one wants!

My old-fashioned fudge is too hard or too soft.

The texture of the fudge is a result of two factors: the cooking temperature, and the amount of stirring it receives. Cooking the fudge even two or three degrees higher or lower than the temperature specified can be the difference between a successful candy and a soupy mess or a rock-hard slab of sugar. Make sure your thermometer is properly calibrated (see page 20) and watch the cooking fudge carefully, so as not to over- or undercook it.

Likewise, there is a fine line between stirring the fudge too much and stirring it too little. If you don't stir enough, the fudge will never set and will have a soft texture more like that of a caramel. If you stir too much, the fudge will harden and set before it can be scraped into the proper pan. It will still taste good, but it's pretty much impossible to cut solidified fudge from a saucepan into beautiful, even squares. The best way to learn when fudge is done is simply to practice, but a good rule of thumb is to watch for it to change from shiny to matte, then immediately scrape it into the pan before it starts to set.

Better Than Grandma's Chocolate Nut Fudge

YIELD: 1 POUND 10 OUNCES (740 G)

8 ounces or 1 cup (235 ml) water

14 ounces or 2 cups (392 g) granulated sugar

2 tablespoons light corn syrup

½ teaspoon salt

11 ounces or 1 cup (308 g) sweetened condensed milk

4 ounces (112 g) unsweetened chocolate, finely chopped

1 tablespoon vanilla extract

1 ounce or 2 tablespoons (28 g) unsalted butter, cubed

4 ounces or 1 cup (112 g) toasted pecans or walnuts, coarsely chopped (see page 33)

Line an 8 x 8-inch (20 x 20-cm) pan with aluminum foil and spray the foil with nonstick cooking spray.

In a 4-quart (3.6-L) saucepan, combine the water, granulated sugar, corn syrup, and salt, and place the pan over medium heat. Stir until the sugar dissolves, then wipe down the sides of the pan with a wet pastry brush to prevent sugar crystals from forming. Bring the syrup to a rolling boil, then stir in the sweetened condensed milk.

After adding the milk, bring the mixture back to a boil, then insert a candy thermometer. Continue to cook the fudge, without stirring, until it reaches 238°F (114°C).

Once at 238°F (114°C), remove the pan from the heat. Sprinkle the chopped chocolate, vanilla extract, and cubed butter on top of the fudge in the pan, but do not stir it in! Just let everything sit on top of the fudge. If you stir right away, you will form sugar crystals that will make your fudge grainy. Instead, let the fudge cool to 120°F (49°C) without disturbing the pan.

When the fudge reaches 120°F (49°C), remove the candy thermometer. Begin to stir the fudge vigorously with a wooden spoon. At first it will be thick and glossy, with a layer of butter on top. But as you continue to stir, the butter will become incorporated and the fudge will become less shiny. After 5 to 10 minutes of stirring it will take on the matte look of chocolate frosting. At this point, the fudge is about to set, so quickly add the chopped nuts and stir them into the fudge. Scrape the fudge into the prepared pan and quickly smooth it into an even layer.

Allow the fudge to set at room temperature, for about 45 minutes. Once set and firm, remove it from the pan and cut the fudge into small 1-inch (2.5-cm) squares to serve. Wrap this fudge well in plastic wrap, and store it in an airtight container in the refrigerator for up to a month. Bring it to room temperature before serving.

ALTERNATIVE METHOD: If you want to save your arm muscles, you can use a stand mixer to beat the fudge instead. After it has reached 238°F (114°C), pour the fudge into a large mixing bowl, but do not scrape the bottom and sides of the bowl when you pour. Add the chocolate, butter, and vanilla on top without stirring, and let the fudge cool to 120°F (49°C) as described above. Once it has reached 120°F (49°C), begin to beat the fudge on medium-low speed with a paddle attachment. It will take about 5 minutes in the mixer for the fudge to reach the thick, matte texture that signals it is finished.

Red Velvet Fudge

YIELD: 2 POUNDS 6 OUNCES (1064 G)

FOR FUDGE

1 pound or 2 cups (470 ml) buttermilk

1⅓ ounces or ⅓ cup (37 g) unsweetened cocoa powder

2¾ ounces or ¼ cup (77 g) light corn syrup

31½ ounces or 4½ cups (882 g) granulated sugar

1 teaspoon salt

½ teaspoon baking soda

4 ounces or 8 tablespoons (112 g) unsalted butter, cubed

2 teaspoons vanilla extract

2 teaspoons red gel food coloring

FOR CREAM CHEESE TOPPING

1½ ounces or 3 tablespoons (42 g) unsalted butter, at room temperature

2 ounces (56 g) cream cheese, at room temperature

½ teaspoon vanilla extract

8 ounces or 2 cups (224 g) powdered sugar, sifted

Pinch of salt

Red sprinkles, for decorating (optional)

Line an 8 x 8-inch (20 x 20-cm) pan with aluminum foil and spray the foil with nonstick cooking spray.

To make the fudge: In a saucepan that holds at least 6 quarts (5.4L), combine the buttermilk, cocoa powder, corn syrup, granulated sugar, salt, and baking soda. Place the pan over medium heat, and whisk everything together until it is combined and there are no lumps of cocoa powder remaining. Continue to stir until all of the sugar is dissolved and the mixture comes to a full boil. It will bubble up a great deal as it cooks.

Wash down the sides of the pan with a wet pastry brush to prevent sugar crystals from forming, and insert a candy thermometer. Boil the candy over medium heat, without stirring, until it reaches 240°F (115°C) on the candy thermometer.

Once at 240°F (115°C), remove the pan from the heat and place the cubed butter, vanilla, and red food coloring on top of the fudge in the pan, but do not stir it in! Just let everything sit on top of the fudge. If you stir right away, you will be forming sugar crystals that will make your fudge grainy. Instead, let the fudge cool to 115°F (46°C) without disturbing the pan.

When the fudge reaches 115°F (46°C), remove the candy thermometer. Begin to stir the fudge vigorously with a wooden spoon. At first it will be thick and glossy, with a layer of butter on top. But as you continue to stir, the butter will become incorporated and the fudge will become less shiny. After 15 to 20 minutes of stirring it will take on the matte look of frosting. At this point, the fudge is about to set, so quickly scrape the fudge into the prepared pan and smooth it into an even layer.

To make the cream cheese topping: In a mixing bowl, combine the softened butter, cream cheese, and vanilla. Beat on medium speed until the mixture is light and there are no lumps of butter or cream cheese. Add the sifted powdered sugar and pinch of salt, and mix on low speed until the powdered sugar is incorporated. Scrape down

the bottom and sides of the bowl, then turn the mixer to medium speed and beat until the topping has a light, fluffy texture.

Scrape the topping onto the red velvet fudge, and smooth it into an even layer. If desired, top the fudge with red sprinkles or red sugar crystals. Refrigerate the fudge to set the topping, for 1 hour. Once set and firm, remove the fudge from the pan and peel off the foil backing. Cut the fudge into small 1-inch (2.5-cm) squares to serve. Store Red Velvet Fudge in an airtight container in the refrigerator for up to 2 weeks. Bring it to room temperature before serving.

—

ALTERNATIVE METHOD: A mixer can be used to beat the fudge instead of doing this step by hand. After it has reached 240°F (116°C), pour the fudge into a large mixing bowl, but do not scrape the bottom and sides of the saucepan when you pour. Add the butter, vanilla, and red food coloring on top without stirring, and let the fudge cool to 115°F (46°C) as described above. Once it has reached 115°F (46°C), begin to beat the fudge on medium-low speed with a paddle attachment. It will take about 10 to 12 minutes in the mixer for the fudge to reach the thick, matte texture that signals it is finished.

Vanilla-Honey Fudge

YIELD: 2 POUNDS 8 OUNCES (1120 G)

2 vanilla beans

4 ounces (112 g) unsalted butter, cubed

6 ounces or ¾ cup (180 g) crème fraîche, not "light" variety (see Note at right)

1 teaspoon salt

6 ounces or ½ cup (168 g) honey

10½ ounces or 1½ cups (294 g) granulated sugar

12 ounces (336 g) white chocolate, chopped, or white chocolate chips

7 ounces or 1¾ cups (196 g) marshmallow creme

Line an 9 x 9-inch (23 x 23-cm) pan with foil and spray the foil with nonstick cooking spray.

Split the vanilla beans lengthwise and scrape out the seeds. Set them aside for now.

In a medium saucepan, combine the butter, crème fraîche, salt, honey, and granulated sugar over medium heat. Stir until the butter melts and the sugar dissolves, then wash down the sides of the pan with a wet pastry brush to prevent sugar crystals from forming.

When the candy comes to a boil, insert a candy thermometer. Continue to cook, stirring occasionally, until the candy reaches 240°F (116°C) on the thermometer.

Once at 240°F (116°C), remove the pan from the heat and add the chopped white chocolate, the marshmallow creme, and the seeds from the vanilla beans. Stir until the white chocolate melts and the fudge is completely smooth.

Pour the fudge into the prepared pan. Let the fudge cool and set at room temperature overnight, or in the refrigerator for at least 3 hours. When set, remove the fudge and peel off the foil backing. Use a large sharp knife to cut the fudge into 1-inch (2.5-cm) pieces to serve. Wrap the fudge well and store it in an airtight container in the refrigerator for up to 2 weeks. This is a soft fudge, so keep it in the refrigerator until serving time.

NOTE

Crème fraîche is a thick French cream similar to sour cream, but with a less tart flavor. It is especially nice for cooking because it gives a rich, full taste but does not curdle when heated (assuming you do not use the "light" variety). If you cannot find crème fraîche at your local grocery store, an equal amount of sour cream can be substituted, but be aware that the flavor will be a bit more assertive.

Peanut Butter Cup Fudge

YIELD: 3 POUNDS (1360 G)

6 ounces or 12 tablespoons
(168 g) unsalted butter, cubed

5¼ ounces or ⅔ cup (147 g)
evaporated whole milk

21 ounces or 3 cups (588 g)
granulated sugar

¾ teaspoon salt

9¾ ounces or 1 cup (273 g)
smooth peanut butter

7 ounces or 2⅓ cups (196 g)
marshmallow creme

1 teaspoon vanilla extract

7 ounces or 1 cup (196 g)
miniature peanut butter cups

Line a 9 x 9-inch (23 x 23-cm) pan with aluminum foil and spray the foil with nonstick cooking spray.

Place the cubed butter in a medium saucepan over medium heat, and gently warm it until it is mostly melted. Once it is almost completely liquid, add the evaporated milk, granulated sugar, and salt, and stir until the sugar dissolves. Wash down the sides of the pan with a wet pastry brush to prevent sugar crystals from forming. Bring the mixture to a boil, and once boiling, insert a candy thermometer. Continue to cook the candy, stirring occasionally, until it reaches 236°F (113°C) on the thermometer.

Once at 236°F (113°C), remove the pan from the heat and add the peanut butter, marshmallow creme, and vanilla. Stir until the peanut butter and marshmallow creme are incorporated and everything is completely smooth.

Pour approximately half of the fudge into the prepared pan and smooth it into an even layer. Working quickly, sprinkle half of the miniature peanut butter cups on top of the fudge in the pan. Pour the remaining fudge into the pan, covering the peanut butter cups, and smooth it into an even layer. Sprinkle the rest of the candies on top of the fudge. Once they come into contact with the hot fudge they will start to melt, so try not to disturb them after you've sprinkled them on, otherwise the chocolate will smear.

Let the fudge cool and set at room temperature overnight, or in the refrigerator for at least 3 hours. When set, remove the fudge and peel off the foil backing. Use a large sharp knife to cut the fudge into 1-inch (2.5-cm) pieces to serve. Wrap the fudge well and store it in an airtight container in the refrigerator for up to 2 weeks. For the best taste and texture, bring it to room temperature before serving.

Grasshopper Fudge

YIELD: 2 POUNDS 4 OUNCES (1134 G)

6 ounces or ¾ cup (168 g)
fat-free evaporated milk

15¾ ounces or 2¼ cups (441 g)
granulated sugar

½ teaspoon salt

10 ounces (280 g) dark
chocolate, chopped

4 ounces or 8 tablespoons
(112 g) unsalted butter, cubed,
at room temperature

1 teaspoon peppermint extract

3½ ounces or 1 cup (98 g)
chocolate-mint cookies,
coarsely chopped

Line an 8 x 8-inch (20 x 20-cm) pan with aluminum foil and spray the foil with nonstick cooking spray.

Place the evaporated milk, granulated sugar, and salt in a medium saucepan over medium-high heat, and stir until the sugar dissolves. Wash down the sides of the pan with a wet pastry brush to prevent sugar crystals from forming. Bring the mixture to a boil, and once boiling, insert a candy thermometer. Continue to cook the candy, stirring continuously, until it reaches 230°F (110°C) on the thermometer.

Once at 230°F (110°C), remove the pan from the heat and add the chocolate, cubed butter, and peppermint extract. Stir until the chocolate and butter melt. Don't worry if the fudge looks broken at this point. Scrape it into a mixing bowl and beat it on low speed for 5 minutes until thick and smooth. Add three-fourths of the chopped cookie pieces and stir them into the fudge.

Scrape the fudge into the prepared pan and smooth it into an even layer. Sprinkle the top of the fudge with the remaining one-fourth chopped cookie pieces. Let the fudge cool and set at room temperature overnight, or in the refrigerator for at least 3 hours. When set, remove the fudge and peel off the foil backing. Use a large sharp knife to cut the fudge into 1-inch (2.5-cm) pieces to serve. Wrap the fudge well and store it in an airtight container in the refrigerator for up to a month. For the best taste and texture, bring it to room temperature before serving.

Candy Bar Fudge

YIELD: 3 POUNDS 8 OUNCES (1568 G)

24 ounces (672 g) dark chocolate, chopped, divided

14 ounces (392 g) sweetened condensed milk

2 ounces or 4 tablespoons (56 g) unsalted butter

½ teaspoon salt

4½ ounces or ¼ cup plus 3 tablespoons (126 g) peanut butter, divided

1 ounce or 1 cup (28 g) crispy rice cereal

14 ounces (392 g) soft caramels, store-bought or homemade (I recommend Sea Salt Caramels, page 66)

7½ ounces or 1½ cups (210 g) toasted, salted peanuts, coarsely chopped (see page 33)

1½ tablespoons corn syrup

3 tablespoons (45 ml) heavy cream, at room temperature

Line a 9 x 9-inch (23 x 23-cm) pan with aluminum foil and spray the foil with nonstick cooking spray.

In a large microwave-safe bowl, combine 18 ounces of the chopped dark chocolate, the sweetened condensed milk, the butter, the salt, and 2½ ounces or ¼ cup (70 g) of the peanut butter. Microwave for 1 minute, then stir. If there are still chunks of chocolate remaining, microwave in 20-second intervals, stirring after every 20 seconds, until the fudge is smooth. Stir in the crispy rice cereal, and scrape the fudge into the prepared pan. Smooth it into an even layer. Refrigerate the fudge for 30 minutes.

To make the nutty caramel layer, place the unwrapped caramels in a microwave-safe bowl. Microwave them in 30-second intervals until they are melted and smooth. Add the chopped peanuts and stir everything together until the peanuts are coated with caramel. Pour the caramel onto the fudge layer and spread it evenly. Refrigerate the fudge for 20 minutes.

To make the chocolate-peanut glaze, combine the remaining 6 ounces (168 g) chocolate, the remaining 2 ounces or 3 tablespoons (56 g) peanut butter, and the corn syrup in a small microwave-safe bowl. Microwave for 30 seconds, then stir everything together. Continue to microwave in 30-second intervals until the chocolate is melted and smooth. Add the room temperature cream and whisk until your glaze is smooth and shiny.

Pour the glaze over the top of the nutty caramel and spread it into a smooth, even layer. Refrigerate the pan to set the fudge, for at least 45 minutes. When set, remove the fudge and peel off the foil backing. Use a large sharp knife to cut the fudge into 1-inch (2.5-cm) pieces to serve. Wrap the fudge well and store it in an airtight container in the refrigerator for up to 1 week. The crispy rice cereal gets soft after this time, but if you omit the cereal the fudge can be easily kept for at least 3 weeks. For the best taste and texture, bring it to room temperature before serving.

CHAPTER 8

Truffles

Truffles are the best con game around. They have a gourmet, elegant, expensive reputation, but in reality they are one of the easiest, most accessible candies to make. The simplest truffle recipes literally have two ingredients, and even the more complex varieties are built on the same basic steps: heat cream. Mix it into chocolate. Stir for a bit, and presto: truffles are born.

Troubleshooting Truffles

My ganache has broken.

Ganache is temperamental, and it can separate as a result of abrupt temperature shifts, overheated chocolate, or the whim of the chocolate gods. Fortunately, it is also fairly easy to repair a broken ganache. If your broken ganache is cool, gently warm the ganache in the microwave or over a water bath. The goal is to get it warm and fluid, not hot, so microwave it in 10-second intervals or keep it on the water bath for 30-second intervals at a time, and whisk between each heating session, until it reaches about 100°F (38°C). Often, reheating the ganache is enough to bring it back together. If this doesn't work, add a teaspoon of room temperature milk to the ganache and continue whisking until it comes together.

If your broken ganache is warm, try whisking it continuously. Often this will make the ganache look worse at first, but after a minute or two of mixing, it will frequently come back together. If it has not come together after several minutes, add a spoonful of room temperature milk and continue whisking until it is no longer broken.

The chocolate coating on my dipped truffles has cracked.

Most of the recipes in this book suggest letting the formed truffles sit overnight in a cool room (63° to 68°F, or 17° to 20°C) before dipping them. This overnight curing period allows the ganache to become firm and dry and form a slight "skin," which makes it easier to dip them at room temperature. Dipping cold truffles in warm chocolate often causes the chocolate to crack, or brings the dipping chocolate out of temper, which is why dipping room temperature truffles is so ideal.

Unfortunately, an overnight truffle curing period is not always feasible given time or weather constraints, so one alternative is to chill the truffles just until they are firm, but not rock-hard or ice-cold. If your chocolate develops cracks, it can sometimes be disguised by a coating of nuts or other embellishments, or a second dip in chocolate once the truffles are at room temperature.

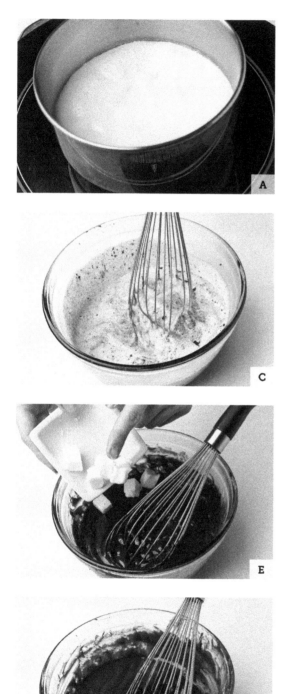

A. Bring the cream to a boil in a small saucepan.

B. Pour the hot cream over the chopped chocolate.

C. After 1 minute, whisk the cream and chocolate together.

D. Stir until the mixture is completely smooth.

E. Add the room temperature butter.

F. Whisk the butter into the ganache until it is smooth and shiny.

How to Make Ganache

The backbone of most truffle recipes is a mixture of chocolate and cream known as ganache. Because truffles are so simple, particular attention should be paid to the quality and selection of the ingredients for the ganache.

The cream you use should be heavy cream—light cream does not contain enough fat, and the taste and texture of the truffles will suffer. Truffles derive most of their flavor from the type of chocolate you use, so always use the best chocolate you can find, and select one whose taste you enjoy on its own. White, milk, and dark chocolates each have different amounts of cocoa solids and should not be used interchangeably in these recipes.

My truffle recipes all include a little corn syrup. It can technically be omitted if you prefer not to cook with corn syrup, but I find even a small amount gives it a smoother, more pleasant texture and adds a touch of sweetness, which is nice when working with dark chocolates. Finally, I like to add a small amount of butter to the finished ganache. Butter gives the truffles a luxurious, melting texture, and makes them taste extra rich.

Each truffle recipe is slightly different, but the basic procedure for making truffles starts with heating the cream. Bring the cream to a boil in a small saucepan. Don't let it continue to boil, or you will cook off too much water and risk breaking your ganache. Place the chopped chocolate in a heat-safe bowl, and pour the hot cream over the chopped chocolate. Let the cream sit and soften the chocolate for 1 minute.

After 1 minute, whisk the cream and chocolate together. Stir until the chocolate has melted and the mixture is completely smooth. Add the room temperature butter, and whisk the butter into the ganache until it is smooth and shiny. Cover the ganache with plastic wrap, and let it cool at room temperature. Once at room temperature, refrigerate the ganache until it is firm enough to scoop.

WHAT DOES IT MEAN WHEN GANACHE "BREAKS"?

Ganache is an emulsion, meaning it is a delicate suspension of fat particles and water. When ganache is properly made it is shiny and smooth, with a thick, puddinglike texture. If the fat separates from the water, the ganache is considered "broken" and will have a grainy, lumpy appearance with a layer of butter resting on top of the chocolate. While broken ganache is technically edible, it's not very appetizing to look at, the texture is unpleasant, and it is difficult to work with. See page 87 for tips on how to salvage broken ganache.

An example of broken ganache on the left, and properly emulsified ganache on the right.

How to Form and Finish Your Truffles

Although truffles originally got their name from their resemblance to the round fungus, they have moved far beyond the basic cocoa powder–dusted ball we're all familiar with. Modern truffles come in a variety of shapes and sizes, from simple chocolate-coated spheres to square truffles to intricately molded pieces of edible art. The recipes in this chapter provide guidelines for how to form and finish your truffles, but they are merely suggestions—let your creativity guide you!

One word of warning: not all ganache recipes are created equal. A ganache designed to fill molded chocolates is typically much looser than the ganache used for round and square truffles. If you want to adapt a regular truffle recipe to use in a molded chocolate, try adding 25 percent more cream to the ganache, to give it a softer, more melting texture. Likewise, you cannot simply roll and dip ganache meant for molding—it will be too soft. If you'd like to adapt a molded ganache recipe, reduce the liquid by about 20 percent to get a ganache that is firm enough to withstand hand-rolling and dipping.

Round Truffles

When it comes to dipping round truffles, you have two options: dipping them by hand, or using dipping tools. Dipping by hand is typically faster and gives the candies a charming old-fashioned appearance, with irregular swirls of chocolate on top. The chocolate coating is often a little thinner on hand-dipped chocolates, which makes it a great method to use if you want to coat your dipped chocolates in cocoa or nuts. If your truffles will be left plain, you might prefer to use dipping

tools to get a smooth, even finish. For ideas for decorating your finished truffles, see page 127.

How to Form Round Truffles

Make sure your chilled ganache is firm enough to hold its shape, but not rock-hard. Use a candy scoop to form small balls of ganache and place them on a sheet of parchment paper. Using a scoop helps ensure each truffle is the same size, but if you don't have a candy scoop you can use a regular spoon.

Dust your hands with a light layer of cocoa powder, and roll the truffles between your palms to get them round. Use a light touch with the cocoa—it is not intended to coat the truffles, it is simply meant to prevent the ganache from sticking to your hands. If possible, let the truffles sit out overnight in a cool room to dry and set the ganache.

How to Hand-Dip Round Truffles

Fill your palm with a spoonful of tempered chocolate. Roll a truffle around your palm until it is coated with chocolate on all sides. If you want to leave your hand-dipped truffles plain, tilt your hand down and let the truffle roll from your palm, down your fingers, onto a sheet of parchment. This action removes excess chocolate and gives the truffle a decorative swirl on top.

If you will be rolling the truffles in cocoa powder, powdered sugar, chopped nuts, or other coatings, roll the chocolate-covered truffle from your palm into the bowl of coating material. Use dipping tools or a fork to turn the truffle and make sure it is completely coated. Let the truffle set for a few

A

B

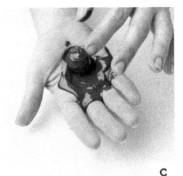

C

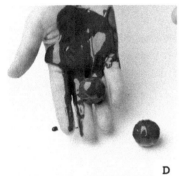

D

E

F

G

H

ROUND TRUFFLES

A. Scoop the truffle into small balls onto a piece of parchment.

B. Roll the truffles between your palms to make them round.

HAND-DIP ROUND TRUFFLES

C. Fill your palm with chocolate, and roll a truffle around in the chocolate until coated.

D. If leaving the truffles plain, roll the truffle from your palm onto a sheet of parchment paper.

E. If coating the truffles, roll the truffle from your palm into a bowl of cocoa powder or your coating of choice.

F. Carefully remove the truffle from the bowl to let the chocolate set completely.

ROUND TRUFFLES WITH DIPPING TOOLS

G. Submerge a truffle completely in chocolate, then pull it out, letting the excess drip back into the bowl.

H. Flip the truffle onto a sheet of parchment.

moments, then remove it from the bowl and place it on a sheet of parchment to set completely.

How to Dip Round Truffles with Dipping Tools

When it comes to dipping truffles, you have your choice of tools. Most sets come with a round or spiral dipper, and a forklike dipper with two or three tines. You can use whichever tool you feel most comfortable with, but if you're just starting out you might find the round dipper is easiest for dipping round truffles. If you don't own dipping tools, you can use a regular fork instead.

Begin by submerging a truffle completely in tempered chocolate. Lift it out of the chocolate, letting the excess drip back into the bowl. Tap the dipping tool against the lip of the bowl to help remove excess chocolate. Flip the truffle upside down onto a sheet of parchment, so that the round dipping tool ends up on top. Repeat until all of the truffles are dipped.

Square Truffles

You don't have to limit yourself to round truffles. Square truffles are chic and modern, and their flat, expansive tops make them a joy to decorate. Any of the round truffles in this chapter can also be used to make square truffles. To really make your square truffles shine, see page 131 for instructions on how to decorate them with chocolate transfer sheets.

How to Form Square Truffles

Spray a square pan with nonstick spray, then press a sheet of plastic wrap into the pan, smoothing out any wrinkles. After the ganache is blended,

pour the still-warm ganache into the prepared pan and smooth it into an even layer. Once it comes to room temperature, place it in the refrigerator to set completely. After the ganache is set, remove it from the pan. Spread a thin layer of melted chocolate on top of the ganache to form the "foot"—a chocolate layer on the bottom of each truffle that makes them easier to dip.

Let the chocolate set completely, then flip the block of ganache upside down so that the foot is on the bottom. Use a large sharp knife to cut the ganache into small squares. If possible, let the truffles sit out overnight to dry and set the ganache.

How to Dip Square Truffles

When dipping square truffles, dipping tools with tines, rather than round tools, should be your weapons of choice. In the absence of legitimate dipping tools, an actual fork can be used with good results. To dip square truffles, begin by submerging a truffle completely in tempered chocolate. Lift it out of the chocolate, letting the excess drip back into the bowl. Gently scrape the bottom of the truffle against the lip of the bowl to remove extra chocolate. Lower the truffle onto a sheet of parchment paper at a slight angle, then slide the tines of the dipping fork out from underneath the truffle.

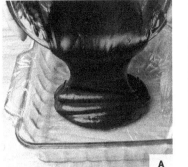
A

B

C

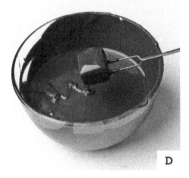
D

E

F

FORMING SQUARE TRUFFLES

A. Line a square pan with plastic wrap, and pour ganache into the pan. Let it set completely.

B. Remove the ganache from the pan and spread melted chocolate in a thin layer on top.

C. Once the chocolate has set, cut the block of ganache into small squares.

DIPPING SQUARE TRUFFLES

D. Submerge a truffle completely in tempered chocolate.

E. Gently scrape the bottom of the truffle against the lip of the bowl.

F. Set the truffle onto a sheet of parchment at an angle.

Classic Chocolate Truffles

YIELD: 48 TRUFFLES

10 ounces (280 g) dark chocolate, finely chopped

8 ounces or 1 cup (235 ml) heavy cream

¾ ounce or 1 tablespoon (21 g) light corn syrup

1 ounce or 2 tablespoons (28 g) unsalted butter, at room temperature

2 ounces or ½ cup (56 g) unsweetened cocoa powder, plus more for dusting

1 pound (454 g) chocolate, melted and tempered (see page 24), for dipping

Place the chopped dark chocolate in a medium bowl. In a small saucepan, combine the heavy cream and the corn syrup and stir them together over medium heat. Bring the cream to a boil, and once it is boiling, immediately pour it over the chopped chocolate in the bowl.

Let the hot cream soften the chocolate for 1 minute, then gently whisk them together. Do not whisk vigorously, or you will incorporate too much air into the ganache. Whisk until all of the chocolate is melted and your ganache is smooth and shiny. Add the room temperature butter and whisk it into the ganache until incorporated. Press a layer of plastic wrap directly on top of the ganache and let it sit until it reaches room temperature.

Once at room temperature, refrigerate the ganache until it is firm enough to scoop into balls, about 2 hours. Use a small 1-inch (2.5-cm) candy scoop to form balls of ganache and place them on a sheet of parchment, as described on page 90. Dust your hands with a light layer of cocoa powder and roll the balls between your palms to get them perfectly round. Let the truffles sit at cool room temperature overnight to dry and set the ganache.

Hand-dip the truffles in the tempered chocolate as described on page 92, and while the chocolate is still wet, roll the truffles in the 2 ounces (56 g) cocoa powder. Store Classic Chocolate Truffles in an airtight container in the refrigerator for up to 2 weeks, and bring them to room temperature before serving.

Mint Chocolate Chip Truffles

YIELD: 36 SMALL TRUFFLES

2⅔ ounces or ⅓ cup (80 ml) heavy cream

12 ounces (336 g) white chocolate, finely chopped

⅛ teaspoon salt

2 ounces or 4 tablespoons (56 g) unsalted butter, at room temperature

1 or 2 drops green food coloring

½ to 1 teaspoon peppermint extract

3½ ounces or ½ cup (98 g) miniature chocolate chips

Powdered sugar, for dusting

1 pound (454 g) chocolate, melted and tempered (see page 24), for dipping

2 ounces (56 g) green candy coating or white chocolate tinted green, for decoration (optional)

Place the cream in a small saucepan over medium heat, and bring it just to a boil. Once boiling, remove the pan from the heat and add the white chocolate to the saucepan, along with the salt. Whisk until the heat from the pan and cream melt the chocolate. The mixture will be very thick. Add the room temperature butter and whisk until the ganache loosens up and is smooth and shiny. Whisk in the green food coloring a drop at a time until you get a light mint color you like.

Add ½ teaspoon of the peppermint extract to the ganache, and taste it to see if the mint flavor is strong enough. Different brands of extract can vary greatly in strength, so it's best to start flavoring conservatively. If you desire a stronger mint flavor, add up to a ½ teaspoon more of the peppermint extract and whisk it in. Pour the ganache into a medium bowl, press a layer of plastic wrap on top of the ganache, and let it cool completely to room temperature.

Once at room temperature, stir in the miniature chocolate chips and refrigerate the ganache until it is firm enough to scoop and roll, about 2 hours. Use a small 1-inch (2.5-cm) candy scoop to form balls of ganache and place them on a sheet of parchment, as described on page 90. Dust your hands with a light layer of powdered sugar and roll the balls between your palms to get them perfectly round. Let the truffles sit at cool room temperature overnight to dry and set the ganache.

Using dipping tools, dip the truffles in the tempered chocolate as described on page 92. Once all of the truffles are dipped, melt the green candy coating or green-tinted white chocolate and drizzle it over the truffles in random swirls, using the technique described on page 127. Let the chocolate set completely. Store Mint Chocolate Chip Truffles in an airtight container in the refrigerator for up to 2 weeks, and let them come to room temperature completely before serving.

Crunchy Hazelnut Truffles

YIELD: 20 TRUFFLES

6 ounces or 1¼ cups (168 g) toasted hazelnuts (see page 33)

5 ounces (140 g) chocolate creme-filled wafer cookies

7 ounces or ⅔ cup (196 g) chocolate-hazelnut spread

1 pound (454 g) chocolate, melted and tempered (see page 24), for dipping

Finely chop ¾ cup (126 g) of the hazelnuts, leaving the remaining ½ cup (42 g) whole (you'll need about 20 whole nuts).

Place the wafer cookies in the bowl of a food processor and pulse them until they are coarsely chopped. Alternately, you can put them in a large zip-top plastic bag and crush them with a rolling pin until the cookies are in small pieces, but are not crushed to dust.

Pour the wafer cookies into a bowl and stir in the chocolate-hazelnut spread. Press a layer of plastic wrap on top of the mixture and refrigerate until it is firm enough to scoop, about 2 hours.

Use a small 1-inch (2.5-cm) scoop to form a ball of candy. Press a whole hazelnut into the center of the ball, and roll it between your palms to get it round. Repeat until all of the candy is formed into balls with hazelnuts in the center. Roll the balls in the crushed hazelnuts to form a coating of nuts on the outside, then roll them between your palms once more to embed the nuts in the chocolate. Refrigerate the truffles until they are very firm.

Using dipping tools, dip the truffles in the tempered chocolate as described on page 90. While the chocolate is still wet, sprinkle the tops with extra chopped hazelnuts remaining from the previous step. Let the chocolate set completely. Store Crunchy Hazelnut Truffles in an airtight container in the refrigerator for up to 2 weeks, and let them come to room temperature completely before serving.

Pink Grapefruit Truffles

YIELD: 36 TRUFFLES

1 pink grapefruit, preferably organic

2⅔ ounces or ⅓ cup (80 ml) heavy cream

9 ounces (252 g) white chocolate, finely chopped

3 ounces (84 g) milk chocolate, finely chopped

⅛ teaspoon salt

1 ounce or 2 tablespoons (28 g) unsalted butter, at room temperature

1 pound (454 g) white chocolate, melted and tempered (see page 24), for dipping

Yellow and pink luster dust, for decoration (optional)

Spray an 8 x 8-inch (20 x 20-cm) pan with nonstick cooking spray and line the pan with plastic wrap.

Use a Microplane to finely zest the grapefruit, and squeeze 2 tablespoons (30 ml) of juice from the grapefruit. Set the juice aside for a moment, and place the zest in a small saucepan along with the heavy cream over medium-high heat. Once it just reaches a boil, remove the pan from the heat, cover it tightly with a lid, and let it sit for 30 minutes to allow the flavor to infuse.

After 30 minutes, remove the lid, return the pan to the heat, and bring the cream back to a boil. Place the chopped white and milk chocolates in a bowl. Pour the cream onto the chopped chocolate through a fine-mesh strainer to strain out the grapefruit zest. Let the cream soften the chocolate for 1 minute, then add the 2 table-spoons (30 ml) grapefruit juice and the salt. Whisk until the chocolates melt and your ganache is smooth. Add the room temperature butter and whisk it in until incorporated. Pour the ganache into the prepared pan, smooth it into an even layer, and refrigerate it until firm, about 90 minutes.

After the ganache is firm, remove it from the pan and peel off the plastic wrap. Spread a few ounces of melted white chocolate evenly on top of the ganache to form a "foot" as described on page 92. Once the chocolate sets, cut the ganache into 36 small squares and let them sit overnight at cool room temperature to dry the ganache.

Using dipping tools, dip the truffles in the tempered white chocolate as described on page 92. Let the chocolate set completely. If you want to decorate the truffles with luster dust, use the dry brush decorating technique as described on page 129. Start brushing yellow dust from one corner of the truffle until you reach the middle of the truffle. Once all of the truffles have yellow luster dust, repeat the process by brushing pink luster dust from the opposite corner, blending the colors in the center of the truffle. Store Pink Grapefruit Truffles in an airtight container in the refrigerator for up to 2 weeks, and let them come to room temperature completely before serving.

Lime Coconut Truffles

YIELD: 36 TRUFFLES

1 large lime, preferably organic

4 ounces or ½ cup (120 ml) heavy cream

2⅔ ounces or 1 cup plus 3 tablespoons (75 g) unsweetened shredded coconut, divided

⅛ teaspoon salt

9 ounces (252 g) white chocolate, finely chopped

2 ounces or 4 tablespoons (56 g) unsalted butter, at room temperature

Powdered sugar, for dusting

1 pound (454 g) white chocolate, melted and tempered (see page 24), for dipping

Use a Microplane to finely zest the lime, and squeeze 1 tablespoon (15 ml) of juice from the lime. Set the juice aside for a moment, and place the zest in a small saucepan along with the heavy cream and 3 tablespoons (12 g) of the shredded coconut. Place the pan over medium-high heat and bring the cream to a boil. Once it just reaches a boil, remove the pan from the heat, cover it tightly with a lid, and let it sit for 30 minutes to allow the lime and coconut flavors to infuse.

Place the chopped white chocolate in a medium bowl. After the cream has infused for 30 minutes, remove the lid, return the pan to the heat, and bring the cream back to a boil. Pour the cream onto the white chocolate through a fine wire-mesh strainer to strain out the lime zest and coconut solids. Let the cream soften the chocolate for 1 minute, then add the salt and 1 tablespoon (15 ml) lime juice, and whisk everything together until the mixture is smooth. Add the room temperature butter and whisk it into the ganache until incorporated. Press a layer of plastic wrap directly on top of the ganache and let it sit until it reaches room temperature.

Once at room temperature, refrigerate the ganache until it is firm enough to scoop into balls, about 2 hours. Use a small 1-inch (2.5-cm) candy scoop to form balls of ganache and place them on a sheet of parchment, as described on page 91. Dust your hands with a light layer of powdered sugar and roll the balls between your palms to get them perfectly round. Let the truffles sit at cool room temperature overnight to dry and set the ganache.

Hand-dip the truffles in the tempered white chocolate as described on page 90, and while the chocolate is still wet, roll the truffles in the remaining 1 cup (63 g) shredded coconut. Store these truffles in an airtight container in the refrigerator for up to 2 weeks, and bring them to room temperature before serving.

Strawberry–Balsamic Vinegar Truffles

YIELD: 40 TRUFFLES

8 ounces (224 g) fresh or frozen strawberries

1 tablespoon (15 ml) heavy cream

1 tablespoon (15 ml) balsamic vinegar

12 ounces (336 g) white chocolate, finely chopped

1 ounce or 2 tablespoons (28 g) unsalted butter, at room temperature

Pink food coloring

Powdered sugar, for dusting

1 pound (454 g) milk chocolate, melted and tempered (see page 24), for dipping

½ ounce or ¼ cup (14 g) finely chopped freeze-dried strawberries, for decoration

Place the strawberries in a saucepan over medium heat and heat them until they release their juices and start to soften. Blend the strawberries, along with their juices, in a blender or food processor. Pour the strawberry purée through a fine-mesh strainer to remove the seeds. Depending on your berries, you will be left with approximately 5 to 6½ ounces or ½ to ⅔ cup (140 to 182 g) strawberry purée.

Pour the purée into a small saucepan and bring it to a simmer. Simmer the purée, stirring frequently, until it reduces to 2½ ounces or ¼ cup (70 g) concentrated strawberry purée. Add the heavy cream and the balsamic vinegar to the concentrated purée, and bring it to a boil.

Place the chopped white chocolate in a medium bowl, and pour the hot strawberry mixture over the chocolate. Let the cream soften the white chocolate for 1 minute, then whisk everything together until the chocolate has melted and the ganache is smooth. The mixture will be very thick. Add the room temperature butter and whisk it into the ganache until incorporated. Add a drop or two of pink food coloring to give your ganache a fresh pink color. Press a layer of plastic wrap directly on top of the ganache and let it sit until it reaches room temperature.

Once at room temperature, refrigerate the ganache until it is firm enough to scoop into balls, about 2 hours. Use a small 1-inch (2.5-cm) candy scoop to form balls of ganache and place them on a sheet of parchment, as described on page 91. Dust your hands with a light layer of powdered sugar and roll the balls between your palms to get them perfectly round. Let the truffles sit at cool room temperature overnight to dry and set the ganache.

Using dipping tools, dip the truffles in the tempered milk chocolate as described on page 92. While the chocolate is still wet, sprinkle the tops with a generous pinch of finely chopped freeze-dried strawberries. Let the chocolate set completely. Store Strawberry–Balsamic Vinegar Truffles in an airtight container in the refrigerator for up to 2 weeks, and let them come to room temperature completely before serving.

Raspberry Rose Truffles

YIELD: 30 TRUFFLES

1½ pounds (681 g) milk chocolate, melted and tempered (see page 24), for molding

8 ounces (224 g) fresh or frozen raspberries

2 ounces or ¼ cup (60 ml) heavy cream

1½ ounces or 2 tablespoons (42 g) light corn syrup

5 ounces (140 g) finely chopped dark chocolate

1 ounce or 2 tablespoons (28 g) unsalted butter, at room temperature

1 teaspoon rose water (see Note below)

Pink luster dust, for decorating

NOTE

Rose water is a common flavoring in Persian desserts, and can often be found in the ethnic food section of many large grocery stores. If you cannot find rose water, a smaller amount of rose candy flavoring or rose oil can be substituted, or you can omit it entirely and enjoy plain raspberry truffles.

Line thirty 1-inch (2.5-cm) chocolate molds with the tempered milk chocolate, as on page 29. Make sure the chocolate lining the molds is completely set.

Place the raspberries in a saucepan over medium heat and heat them until they release their juices. Blend the raspberries, along with their juices, in a blender or food processor. Pour the raspberry purée through a fine-mesh strainer to remove the seeds.

Pour the purée into a small saucepan and bring it to a simmer. Simmer the purée, stirring frequently, until it reduces to 2½ ounces or ¼ cup (70 g) concentrated raspberry purée. Add the heavy cream and light corn syrup to the purée and stir everything together. Bring the mixture just to a boil.

Place the chopped dark chocolate in a medium bowl, and pour the hot raspberry mixture over the chocolate. Let the cream soften the chocolate for 1 minute, then whisk everything together until the chocolate has melted. Add the room temperature butter and whisk it into the ganache until incorporated, then whisk in the rose water. Press a layer of plastic wrap directly on top of the ganache and let it sit until it reaches room temperature.

Spoon or pipe the room temperature ganache into the prepared chocolate molds, being sure to leave room at the top to seal the molds with chocolate. Once the molds are filled, refrigerate the molds for 45 minutes, until the ganache mixture is firm.

Seal the tops of the molds with the tempered milk chocolate and let the chocolate set for 45 minutes at room temperature. Once set, carefully remove the chocolates from the molds. Decorate them with pink luster dusting using the dry brush technique described on page 129.

Store Raspberry Rose Truffles in an airtight container in the refrigerator for up to 2 weeks, and allow them to come to room temperature before serving.

Almond Amaretti Truffles

YIELD: 26 TRUFFLES

4 ounces (112 g) amaretti cookies (see Note below)

7 ounces (196 g) almond paste

2⅔ ounces or ⅓ cup (80 ml) heavy cream

12 ounces (336 g) dark chocolate, finely chopped

Cocoa powder, for dusting

1 pound (454 g) dark chocolate, melted and tempered (see page 24), for dipping

Place the amaretti cookies in the bowl of a food processor and blend into very fine crumbs. Alternately, place them in a zip-top plastic bag and crush them with a rolling pin until the cookies are fine crumbs.

Finely chop the almond paste or grate it using a cheese grater. Combine the chopped almond paste, the cream, and the chopped dark chocolate in a large microwave-safe bowl. Microwave in 30-second intervals, stirring after every 30 seconds, until the chocolate melts, the almond paste dissolves, and the mixture is fluid and shiny. Because of the almond paste, there will be a slightly grainy texture to the ganache at this point, but the addition of the crunchy cookies will eliminate any textural problems. Add 1½ ounces or ¼ cup (42 g) of the crushed amaretti cookies to the ganache and stir everything together. Reserve the rest of the cookie crumbs for finishing the truffles. Press a layer of plastic wrap directly on top of the ganache and let it sit until it reaches room temperature.

Once at room temperature, refrigerate the ganache until it is firm enough to scoop into balls, about 1 hour. Use a small 1-inch (2.5-cm) candy scoop to form balls of ganache and place them on a sheet of parchment, as described on page 90. Dust your hands with a light layer of cocoa powder and roll the balls between your palms to get them perfectly round. Let the truffles sit at cool room temperature overnight to dry and set the ganache.

Hand-dip the truffles in the tempered dark chocolate as described on page 90, and while the chocolate is still wet, roll the truffles in the remaining crushed amaretti cookies. Store Almond Amaretti Truffles in an airtight container in the refrigerator for up to 2 weeks, and bring them to room temperature before serving.

> **NOTE**
>
> Amaretti cookies can be found in many gourmet supermarkets, Italian delis, or online shops.

CHAPTER 9

Chocolate Candies

I cannot argue with the simple appeal of a bar of solid chocolate, but sometimes chocolate is best enjoyed in combination with other flavors and textures. Eating a whole slab of chocolate in one sitting can be daunting, but when that chocolate is studded with salty nuts or crispy toffee, well . . . somehow that bar miraculously disappears in record time.

In this chapter, chocolate is paired with an assortment of different fruits, nuts, candies, and even cookies to make easy, crowd-pleasing barks, clusters, and more. Rather than masking the taste of the chocolate, these mix-ins highlight chocolate's flavor and versatility. Most of the recipes require minimal time and preparation, so this chapter is a good place to start if you're new to chocolate making or if you're simply short on time and need a chocolate fix in a hurry.

Troubleshooting Chocolate Candies

My chocolate gets too thick when I add my mix-ins.

If your chocolate is already on the low end of the workable range for tempered chocolate, adding other ingredients can cause it to cool too quickly and set in the bowl. When making barks or clusters, monitor the temperature of your chocolate to make sure it is in the workable range, and make sure that any ingredients you add are at room temperature.

My chocolate candies are streaky, spotted, or soft at room temperature.

These are all classic signs of chocolate "bloom," meaning that your chocolate was not tempered properly. There is nothing that can be done to change the chocolates once they have been formed, but refer to page 24 for tempering instructions to avoid this problem in the future.

Sweet and Salty Bark

YIELD: 1 POUND 12 OUNCES (784 G)

4 ounces or about 1½ cups (112 g) chopped pretzel twists

6 ounces or about 1 cup (168 g) chopped toffee bits

18 ounces (504 g) dark or milk chocolate, melted and tempered (see page 24)

Flaked sea salt, for finishing

Cover a baking sheet with a layer of aluminum foil or parchment paper. Set aside ¼ cup (20 g) of the pretzels and ¼ cup (42 g) of the toffee bits, and stir the remaining 1¼ cups (92 g) pretzels and ¾ cup (126 g) toffee bits into the melted, tempered chocolate.

Scrape the chocolate out onto the prepared pan, and spread it into a thin layer a little more than ¼ inch (6 mm) thick. It does not have to cover the entire baking sheet.

While the chocolate is still wet, sprinkle the reserved pretzel pieces and toffee over the top of the chocolate, and press down gently to adhere them to the chocolate. Top the bark with a generous sprinkling of flaked sea salt.

Let the bark set at room temperature for 45 minutes, or in the refrigerator for 15 minutes. Once it is completely set, break the bark apart into small pieces by hand. Store Sweet and Salty Bark in an airtight container at cool room temperature for up to a month.

Zebra Bark

YIELD: 1 POUND 4 OUNCES (560 G)

12 ounces (336 g) dark chocolate, melted and tempered (see page 24)

4 ounces (112 g) white chocolate, melted and tempered (see page 24)

2 ounces or ⅓ cup (56 g) chocolate-covered peanuts

2½ ounces or ⅓ cup (70 g) yogurt-covered raisins

Cover a baking sheet with a layer of aluminum foil or parchment paper. Pour the tempered dark chocolate onto the sheet, and spread it into a thin layer about ¼ inch (6 mm) thick. It doesn't need to cover the entire baking sheet.

While the dark chocolate is still wet, pour the tempered white chocolate into a zip-top plastic bag and cut a small hole in one corner for the chocolate to flow through. (Alternately, you can use a pastry bag fitted with a small round tip.) Starting at the top of the dark chocolate, draw white chocolate lines across the width of the chocolate, spacing them about ½ inch (1.3 cm) apart. Continue until you have drawn lines across the whole slab of chocolate.

Drag a toothpick through both chocolates, starting at the top corner and pulling the toothpick down the length of the chocolate. When you get to the bottom, move the toothpick over ¼ inch (6 mm) and drag it upward, creating a chevron design in the chocolate. Continue swirling the chocolate together in an up-and-down pattern until all of the chocolate is swirled in a zebra pattern.

Scatter the chocolate-covered peanuts and the yogurt-covered raisins over the top of the bark, gently pressing them down to adhere them to the chocolate.

Let the bark set at room temperature for 45 minutes, or in the refrigerator for 15 minutes. Once it is completely set, break the bark apart into small pieces by hand. Store Zebra Bark at cool room temperature for up to a month.

—

VARIATION: There are many different varieties of chocolate- and yogurt-covered fruit and nuts, so feel free to experiment with substituting other nuts or fruit for the peanuts and raisins in the recipe. Just be sure to keep to the black and white color scheme!

Ice Cream Sundae Bark

YIELD: 1 POUND 4 OUNCES (560 G)

2½ ounces or ⅓ cup (70 g) coarsely chopped maraschino cherries

1 vanilla bean (optional, for a stronger vanilla flavor)

12 ounces (336 g) white chocolate, melted and tempered (see page 26)

1½ ounces or ¼ cup (42 g) chopped toffee bits

1½ ounces or ¼ cup (42 g) chopped salted peanuts

1 ounce (28 g) dark chocolate, melted (see page 26)

1 ounce or 3 tablespoons (28 g) colored sprinkles

Spread the chopped maraschino cherries out onto a length of paper towel and carefully and thoroughly pat them dry. Cover a baking sheet with a layer of aluminum foil or parchment paper.

If you are using the vanilla bean, split it in half lengthwise with a sharp paring knife. Scrape out the seeds from the bean and add the seeds to the white chocolate, stirring until they are thoroughly mixed in.

Set aside 2 tablespoons (21 g) each of the chopped toffee bits and chopped salted peanuts. Stir the remaining 2 tablespoons (21 g) of the toffee and nuts into the tempered white chocolate. Scrape the chocolate onto the prepared baking sheet and spread it into a thin, even layer. It does not need to cover the entire sheet.

While the white chocolate is still wet, drizzle the melted dark chocolate on top in a random, swirling pattern. Sprinkle the reserved chopped toffee and peanuts on top, then scatter the colored sprinkles all over the top of the bark. Finally, sprinkle the chopped maraschino cherries over the top. Gently press down on the cherries to adhere them to the melted chocolate.

Let the bark set at room temperature for 45 minutes, or in the refrigerator for 15 minutes. Once it is completely set, break the bark apart into small pieces by hand. Store Ice Cream Sundae Bark in the refrigerator for up to 2 weeks.

—

VARIATIONS: There are many other ice cream–themed ingredients you could add to this bark! Consider including a handful of chopped caramel pieces, miniature marshmallows, or chopped banana chips to the melted white chocolate.

Sour Cherry and Macadamia Nut Clusters

YIELD: 24 CANDIES

3 ounces or ½ cup (84 g) coarsely chopped tart dried cherries (see Note)

3 ounces or ½ cup (84 g) coarsely chopped salted macadamia nuts

⅔ ounce or ½ cup (19 g) chopped meringue cookies

12 ounces (336 g) dark chocolate, melted and tempered (see page 26)

Cover a baking sheet with a layer of aluminum foil or parchment paper.

Add the chopped dried cherries, the chopped macadamia nuts, and the chopped meringue cookies to the tempered chocolate, and stir until all of the ingredients are well distributed and coated with chocolate.

Using a teaspoon or a small candy scoop, drop spoonfuls of the chocolate mixture onto the prepared baking sheet. Once all of the clusters are formed, let them set at room temperature for about 30 minutes, or in the refrigerator for 15 minutes.

Store Sour Cherry and Macadamia Nut Clusters at cool room temperature for up to a month.

NOTE

Tart dried cherries are different from regular dried cherries, which are much sweeter. If you can't find tart dried cherries, dried cranberries are a good substitute.

Chocolate Medallions

YIELD: 24 CANDIES

⅔ ounce (19 g) or about 4 large strips candied orange peel

10 ounces (280 g) dark or milk chocolate, melted and tempered (see page 24)

1½ ounces or ¼ cup (42 g) toasted, salted pistachios (see page 31)

1½ ounces or ¼ cup (42 g) dried cranberries

Cover a baking sheet with aluminum foil or parchment paper. Cut the candied orange peel into small pieces about the size of the pistachios and cranberries.

Use a large spoon to drop a dollop of chocolate onto the baking sheet. Gently nudge it outward in a circle until the chocolate disk is about 1½ inches (3.8 cm) in diameter. Form two more circles, then carefully place an assortment of the pistachios, cranberries, and slivered orange peel on top of the chocolate disks. The toppings should look deliberate, not jumbled together, so aim for five or six well-placed pieces per disk.

Repeat this process, making about three medallions at a time, until you've run out of chocolate and toppings. Let the medallions set at room temperature for about 30 minutes. Store them between layers of waxed paper or parchment paper at cool room temperature for up to a month.

Chocolate Peanut Butter Cups

YIELD: 24 PEANUT BUTTER CUPS

12 ounces (336 g) dark or milk chocolate, melted and tempered (see page 24)

9½ ounces or 1 cup (266 g) smooth peanut butter

2¼ ounces or ½ cup (60 g) sifted powdered sugar

¼ teaspoon salt

¾ ounce or ¼ cup (21 g) graham cracker crumbs (from about 1½ crushed graham crackers)

Lay out 24 small candy cups on your work surface. Working with three or four cups at a time, spoon a bit of chocolate into each cup so that they are approximately one-quarter full (**A**, on page 111). Use a small, clean, food-safe paintbrush to brush the tempered chocolate up the sides of each cup in a smooth, even layer (**B**, on page 111). Make sure the sides are completely covered, and periodically hold a cup up to the light to see if there are any translucent areas that need to be covered with a thicker layer of chocolate. Repeat until all of your cups are lined with chocolate. You will have extra chocolate left over for covering the top later on. Refrigerate the chocolate shells until they are set.

While the chocolate is firming up, make the peanut butter filling. In a medium bowl, combine the peanut butter, powdered sugar, salt, and graham cracker crumbs. Stir until the filling is smooth and there are no dry pockets of sugar or crumbs.

Once the shells are firm, fill them with the peanut butter mixture. You can either spoon it in or use a pastry bag fitted with a ½-inch (1.3-cm) round tip to pipe peanut butter filling into the chocolate shells (**C**, on page 111). Leave at least ⅛ inch (3 mm) between the filling and the top of the chocolate cup, so that they can be covered with chocolate.

If necessary, re-warm the extra chocolate. Spoon a bit of chocolate onto the top of each cup and gently tilt the cup or nudge the chocolate with your spoon so that it covers all of the peanut butter and forms a tight seal with the sides of the chocolate cup (**D**, on page 111).

Let the chocolate set completely at room temperature for 30 minutes, or in the refrigerator for 15 minutes. Store Chocolate Peanut Butter Cups in an airtight container at room temperature for up to a month.

(continued on next page)

The Beginner's Guide to Candy Making

VARIATIONS: Virtually any nut or seed butter can be substituted for peanut butter in this recipe, and chocolate-nut spreads and cookie-based spreads are a more indulgent substitute. If you are using a sweet spread, consider reducing the sugar and increasing the graham cracker crumbs to prevent the filling from becoming too sweet.

These chocolate cups can also be used with a number of other fillings, like a soft caramel or a loose ganache. You can even use these to make petit fours by adding a swirl of mousse, a dollop of whipped cream, or a spoonful of ice cream.

A. Fill the candy cups one-quarter full of tempered chocolate.

B. Use a small, food-safe paintbrush to brush the chocolate up the sides of the cups.

C. After the chocolate has set, spoon or pipe your filling into the cups, leaving space at the top.

D. Cover the cups with melted chocolate, making sure it covers all of the filling.

CHAPTER 10

Marshmallows

Freshly made marshmallows bear little relation to their sad, store-bought cousins. If your only exposure to marshmallows has been in the form of stale cylinders tasting vaguely of artificial vanilla, you are in for a treat! Homemade marshmallows are light and fluffy, with a pillowy texture that melts in the mouth. These are marshmallows you'll want to eat plain, but if you're able to resist eating the whole pan, they're also excellent in hot chocolate and any number of baking recipes. Very Vanilla Marshmallows (page 115) are the perfect all-purpose marshmallow, but if you're ready for more adventurous flavors, I urge you to try your hand at chocolate, Neapolitan, or fruit-flavored marshmallows.

Troubleshooting Marshmallows

My egg whites are liquid even after whipping them in the mixer—they will not form firm peaks.

Egg whites won't whip properly if they come into contact with any fat. This includes bits of the egg yolk that might be left in the whites, or any residual grease in the mixing bowl. For the best results, make sure your egg whites are at room temperature, and that there are no specks of egg yolk in the whites. Wash and dry the mixing bowl very thoroughly to remove all traces of grease before whipping egg whites.

My marshmallows are too stiff to scrape into the pan.

The marshmallows have likely been overbeaten, and the gelatin has started to set, resulting in a stiff, lumpy texture that won't make appealing marshmallows. You can try to save them by placing the mixing bowl over a water bath full of simmering water, and stirring until the marshmallow loosens up. Immediately pour the marshmallow into your pan and smooth it into an even layer.

My marshmallows have set, but they are too soft and sticky.

Overly soft and sticky marshmallows can be caused by a variety of factors. If you tried to make the marshmallows on a humid or stormy day, the weather could be to blame. Marshmallows are best made on days with low humidity. Another possibility is that the sugar syrup was not cooked to a high enough temperature—next time, calibrate your thermometer before beginning (see page 20) and be sure to cook the syrup to the temperature specified in the recipe. Finally, you just may have a personal preference for very firm marshmallows, in which case you should increase the amount of gelatin in the recipe to get a firmer marshmallow.

A

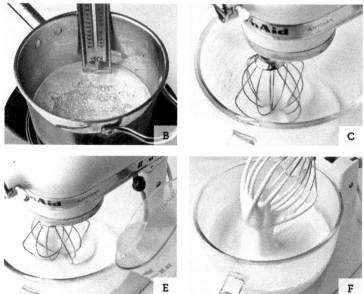
B

C

D

E

F

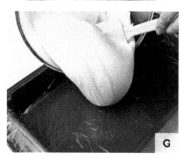
G

H

I

HOW TO MAKE MARSHMALLOWS

Every marshmallow recipe is a little different, but here is a general guide for making homemade marshmallows.

A. Whisk the gelatin into cold water and let it sit until the water is absorbed.

B. Combine the ingredients for the sugar syrup and cook it to the specified temperature.

C. While the sugar syrup boils, whip the egg whites until firm peaks form.

D. Heat the gelatin until it is liquid, and whisk together the liquid gelatin and the hot sugar syrup.

E. With the mixer running, pour the sugar syrup into the egg whites.

F. Increase the speed to high and beat the marshmallow until it is very thick and shiny and forms a thick ribbon when you lift the beater. Add any colorings or flavorings and mix them in.

G. Scrape the marshmallow into the prepared pan and smooth it into an even layer. Let it set undisturbed overnight.

H. Dust the marshmallow with powdered sugar and cut it into small squares.

I. Dredge the squares in powdered sugar to prevent them from sticking together.

Very Vanilla Marshmallows

YIELD: 1 POUND 6 OUNCES (616 G)

2½ ounces (70 g) or 2 large egg whites, at room temperature

8 ounces or 1 cup (235 ml) cold water, divided

¾ ounce (21 g) or 3 (¼-ounce, or 7-g) envelopes unflavored gelatin

14 ounces or 2 cups (392 g) granulated sugar

5½ ounces or ½ cup (154 g) light corn syrup

¼ teaspoon salt

1 ounce or 2 tablespoons (28 g) vanilla bean paste (see Note on page 116)

4 ounces or 1 cup (112 g) powdered sugar

Line a 9 x 13-inch (23 x 33-cm) baking pan with aluminum foil or plastic wrap, and spray the foil or plastic wrap with nonstick cooking spray.

Place the room temperature egg whites in the bowl of a large stand mixer fitted with a whisk attachment.

Pour ½ cup (118 ml) of the cold water into a small bowl, and whisk in the gelatin. Set the bowl aside to let the gelatin "bloom," or absorb the water.

Pour the remaining ½ cup (118 ml) water into a medium heavy-bottomed saucepan, and stir in the granulated sugar, the light corn syrup, and the salt. Place the pan over medium-high heat and continue to stir until the sugar dissolves. Brush down the sides of the pan with a wet pastry brush to remove any stray sugar crystals. Insert a candy thermometer.

Cook the sugar syrup, without stirring, until the thermometer reaches 260°F (127°C). This will take 10 to 15 minutes, so while you're waiting for the sugar to cook, microwave the gelatin bowl for about 20 seconds, until the gelatin liquefies.

When the sugar syrup reaches 245°F (118°C), begin beating the egg whites on medium speed. The egg whites should be well beaten and be able to hold firm peaks at approximately the same time the sugar syrup reaches 260°F (127°C).

When the sugar syrup is at 260°F (127°C), remove the pan from the heat and carefully whisk in the liquid gelatin mixture. It will bubble up and steam a bit, so watch your hands during this step.

(continued on next page)

The hot sugar syrup now needs to be added to the egg whites. If your saucepan does not have a spout, pour the syrup into a large mixing cup or pitcher with a spout, to give you more control over the process. Turn the mixer to low, and with the mixer running, slowly stream the hot sugar syrup into the beaten egg whites. Try to pour the syrup close to the sides of the bowl, so it doesn't hit the whisk and splatter everywhere.

Once all of the syrup is added to the whites, gradually increase the speed of the mixer until it is running on medium-high speed. Whip the marshmallow until it is very thick, shiny, and opaque, about 8 to 10 minutes, depending on your mixer. When you lift the whisk from the marshmallow, it should slowly stream from the whisk in a thick ribbon. Add the vanilla bean paste and mix the marshmallow for another 20 seconds to distribute the paste.

Pour the marshmallow into the prepared pan and smooth it into an even layer. Let the marshmallow sit and rest, undisturbed, at room temperature until it is completely set, about 8 hours.

When you're ready to cut the marshmallow, dust your work surface with powdered sugar, and sprinkle a layer of powdered sugar on top of the marshmallow. Flip the marshmallow facedown onto the work surface and peel the foil or plastic wrap off the back. Dust a large chef's knife with powdered sugar and cut the marshmallow into long thin strips, cleaning the knife frequently as it gets sticky. Cut the strips of marshmallow into small squares. Toss the marshmallow squares in powdered sugar to prevent them from sticking together. Store the marshmallows in an airtight container at room temperature for up to 2 weeks.

—

VARIATION: To make other flavors of marshmallow, omit the vanilla bean paste and add 1 to 2 teaspoons of a flavoring extract, depending on the strength of the extract.

NOTE

Vanilla bean paste is a favorite ingredient of pastry chefs, and it is becoming more common in household pantries as well. It's a thick paste full of vanilla seeds, with a bold flavor and a beautiful vanilla-speckled appearance. For ideas on where to find vanilla bean paste, see the Resources section on page 140. If you don't have the paste, you can substitute seeds scraped from 2 vanilla pods, or 2 tablespoons (30 ml) vanilla extract.

Dark Chocolate Marshmallows

YIELD: 1 POUND 6 OUNCES (616 G)

11 ounces or 1¼ cup plus 2 tablespoons (325 ml) cold water, divided

2⅓ ounces or ⅓ cup plus ¼ cup (65 g) unsweetened cocoa powder, divided

¾ ounce (21 g) or 3 (¼-ounce, or 7-g) envelopes unflavored gelatin

14 ounces or 2 cups (392 g) granulated sugar

8¼ ounces or ¾ cup (231 g) light corn syrup

3 ounces or ¾ cup (84 g) powdered sugar

Line a 9 x 9-inch (23 x 23-cm) baking pan with aluminum foil or plastic wrap, and spray the foil or plastic wrap with nonstick cooking spray.

Heat ¼ cup plus 2 tablespoons (90 ml) of the water in a small bowl in the microwave for 2 minutes. Add 1⅓ ounces or ⅓ cup (37 g) of the cocoa powder to the hot water and whisk until the cocoa dissolves, then set aside.

Pour ½ cup (120 ml) of the cold water into the bowl of a stand mixer. Sprinkle the gelatin on top and whisk it in.

In a medium saucepan, combine the remaining ½ cup (120 ml) water, the granulated sugar, and the corn syrup. Place the pan over medium-high heat and stir until the sugar dissolves. Brush down the sides of the pan with a wet pastry brush to remove any stray sugar crystals, and insert a candy thermometer. Cook the sugar syrup, without stirring, until the thermometer reaches 250°F (121°C).

When the sugar syrup is almost done cooking, add the cocoa mixture to the gelatin and mix them together on low speed. Once the sugar syrup reaches 250°F (121°C), the syrup now needs to be added to the gelatin. If your saucepan does not have a spout, pour the syrup into a large mixing cup or pitcher with a spout, to give you more control over the process. Turn the mixer to low, and with the mixer running, slowly stream the hot sugar syrup into the gelatin. Try to pour the syrup close to the sides of the bowl, so it doesn't hit the whisk and splatter everywhere.

(continued on next page)

Once all of the syrup is added to the mixing bowl, gradually increase the speed of the mixer until it is running on medium-high speed. Whip the marshmallow until it is very thick, shiny, and opaque, about 8 to 10 minutes, depending on your mixer. When you lift the whisk from the marshmallow, it should slowly stream from the whisk in a thick ribbon.

Pour the marshmallow into the prepared pan and smooth it into an even layer. Let the marshmallow sit and rest, undisturbed, at room temperature until it is completely set, about 8 hours.

When you're ready to cut the marshmallow, mix together the remaining ¼ cup (28 g) cocoa powder and the powdered sugar, and sprinkle this mixture on top of the marshmallow. Flip the marshmallow facedown onto the work surface and peel the foil or plastic wrap off the back. Dust a large chef's knife with the powdered sugar and cocoa mixture and cut the marshmallow into long thin strips, cleaning the knife frequently as it gets sticky. Cut the strips of marshmallow into small squares. Toss the marshmallow squares in the powdered sugar and cocoa mixture to prevent them from sticking together. Store the marshmallows in an airtight container at room temperature for up to 2 weeks.

Peppermint Swirl Marshmallows

YIELD: 1 POUND 6 OUNCES (616 G)

2½ ounces (70 g) or 2 large egg whites, at room temperature

8 ounces or 1 cup (235 ml) cold water, divided

¾ ounce (21 g) or 3 (¼-ounce, or 7-g) envelopes unflavored gelatin

14 ounces or 2 cups (392 g) granulated sugar

5½ ounces or ½ cup (154 g) light corn syrup

¼ teaspoon salt

½ to 1 teaspoon peppermint extract

Red gel food coloring

4 ounces or 1 cup (112 g) powdered sugar

Line a 9 x 13-inch (23 x 33-cm) baking pan with aluminum foil or plastic wrap, and spray the foil or plastic wrap with nonstick cooking spray.

Place the room temperature egg whites in the bowl of a large stand mixer fitted with a whisk attachment.

Pour ½ cup (120 ml) of the cold water into a small bowl, and whisk in the gelatin. Set the bowl aside to let the gelatin "bloom," or absorb the water.

Pour the remaining ½ cup (120 ml) water into a medium heavy-bottomed saucepan, and stir in the granulated sugar, the light corn syrup, and the salt. Place the pan over medium-high heat and continue to stir until the sugar dissolves. Brush down the sides of the pan with a wet pastry brush to remove any stray sugar crystals. Insert a candy thermometer.

Cook the sugar syrup, without stirring, until the thermometer reaches 260°F (127°C). This will take 10 to 15 minutes, so while you're waiting for the sugar to cook, microwave the gelatin bowl for about 20 seconds, until the gelatin liquefies.

When the sugar syrup reaches 245°F (118°C), begin beating the egg whites on medium speed. The egg whites should be well beaten and be able to hold firm peaks at approximately the same time the sugar syrup reaches 260°F (127°C).

When the sugar syrup is at 260°F (127°C), remove the pan from the heat and carefully whisk in the liquid gelatin mixture. It will bubble up and steam a bit, so watch your hands during this step.

(continued on next page)

The hot sugar syrup now needs to be added to the egg whites. If your saucepan does not have a spout, pour the syrup into a large mixing cup or pitcher with a spout, to give you more control over the process. Turn the mixer to low, and with the mixer running, slowly stream the hot sugar syrup into the beaten egg whites. Try to pour the syrup close to the sides of the bowl, so it doesn't hit the whisk and splatter everywhere.

Once all of the syrup is added to the whites, gradually increase the speed of the mixer until it is running on medium-high speed. Whip the marshmallow until it is very thick, shiny, and opaque, about 8 to 10 minutes, depending on your mixer. When you lift the whisk from the marshmallow, it should slowly stream from the whisk in a thick ribbon. Add ½ teaspoon of the peppermint extract and mix for 20 seconds to incorporate it. Taste the marshmallow, and if you would like a stronger mint flavor, mix in the remaining ½ teaspoon peppermint extract.

Pour the marshmallow into the prepared pan and smooth it into an even layer. Drizzle the red food coloring over the top of the marshmallow in a random pattern. Drag a toothpick through the marshmallow, swirling the food coloring on top. Stop before the colors start to bleed, while you still have distinct red and white swirls. Let the marshmallow sit and rest, undisturbed, at room temperature until it is completely set, about 8 hours.

When you're ready to cut the marshmallow, dust your work surface with the powdered sugar, and sprinkle a layer of powdered sugar on top of the marshmallow. Flip the marshmallow facedown onto the work surface and peel the foil or plastic wrap off the back. Dust a large chef's knife with powdered sugar and cut the marshmallow into long thin strips, cleaning the knife frequently as it gets sticky. Cut the strips of marshmallow into small squares. Toss the marshmallow squares in powdered sugar to prevent them from sticking together. Store the marshmallows in an airtight container at room temperature for up to 2 weeks.

Neapolitan Marshmallows

YIELD: 1 POUND 12 OUNCES (794 G)

FOR CHOCOLATE MARSHMALLOW LAYER

1¼ ounces (35 g) or 1 large egg white, at room temperature

6 ounces or ¾ cup (180 ml) water, divided

⅓ ounce or 1 tablespoon (9 g) unflavored gelatin

7 ounces or 1 cup (196 g) granulated sugar

¾ ounce or 1 tablespoon (21 g) light corn syrup

¼ ounce or 1 tablespoon (7 g) unsweetened cocoa powder

(continued on next page)

Line a 9 x 13-inch (23 x 33-cm) baking pan with aluminum foil or plastic wrap, and spray the foil or plastic wrap with nonstick cooking spray.

To make the chocolate marshmallow layer: Place the room temperature egg white in the bowl of a large stand mixer fitted with a whisk attachment.

Pour ¼ cup (60 ml) of the cold water into a small bowl, and whisk in the gelatin. Set the bowl aside to let the gelatin "bloom," or absorb the water.

Pour the remaining ½ cup (120 ml) water into a medium heavy-bottomed saucepan, and stir in the granulated sugar and the light corn syrup. Place the pan over medium-high heat and continue to stir until the sugar dissolves. Brush down the sides of the pan with a wet pastry brush to remove any stray sugar crystals. Insert a candy thermometer.

Cook the sugar syrup, without stirring, until the thermometer reaches 260°F (127°C). While you're waiting for the sugar to cook, microwave the gelatin bowl for about 20 seconds, until the gelatin liquefies.

When the sugar syrup reaches 245°F (118°C), begin beating the egg white on medium speed. The egg white should be well beaten and be able to hold firm peaks at approximately the same time the sugar syrup reaches 260°F (127°C).

When the sugar syrup is at 260°F (127°C), remove the pan from the heat and carefully whisk in the liquid gelatin mixture. It will bubble up and steam a bit, so watch your hands during this step.

The hot sugar syrup now needs to be added to the egg white. If your saucepan does not have a spout, pour the syrup into a large mixing cup or pitcher with a spout, to give you more control over the

(continued on next page)

FOR VANILLA MARSHMALLOW LAYER

1¼ ounces (35 g) or 1 large egg white, at room temperature

6 ounces or ¾ cup (180 ml) water, divided

⅓ ounce or 1 tablespoon (9 g) unflavored gelatin

7 ounces or 1 cup (196 g) granulated sugar

¾ ounce or 1 tablespoon (21 g) light corn syrup

1 teaspoon vanilla extract

FOR STRAWBERRY MARSHMALLOW LAYER

1¼ ounces (35 g) or 1 large egg white, at room temperature

6 ounces or ¾ cup (180 ml) water, divided

⅓ ounce or 1 tablespoon (9 g) unflavored gelatin

7 ounces or 1 cup (196 g) granulated sugar

¾ ounce or 1 tablespoon (21 g) light corn syrup

¼ to 1 teaspoon strawberry extract

Pink food coloring

4 ounces or 1 cup (112 g) powdered sugar

process. Turn the mixer to low, and with the mixer running, slowly stream the hot sugar syrup into the beaten egg whites. Try to pour the syrup close to the sides of the bowl, so it doesn't hit the whisk and splatter everywhere.

Once all of the syrup is added to the whites, gradually increase the speed of the mixer until it is running on medium-high speed. Whip the marshmallow until it is very thick, shiny, and opaque, about 10 to 12 minutes, depending on your mixer. When you lift the whisk from the marshmallow, it should slowly stream from the whisk in a thick ribbon. Sift in the cocoa powder and mix for 20 seconds until it is well distributed.

Scrape the marshmallow into the prepared pan and smooth it into an even layer.

Repeat this process **to make the vanilla marshmallow layer**, adding vanilla extract instead of cocoa powder once the marshmallow has been whipped. Spread the vanilla marshmallow on top of the chocolate marshmallow layer.

Finally, repeat this process once more **to make the strawberry marshmallow.** When you add the strawberry extract at the end, begin by adding only ¼ teaspoon. Different flavorings have very different strengths, and it's important to start with a small amount in case yours is very strong. Taste the marshmallow, and add more extract if desired. Add a drop or two of pink food coloring, and mix the marshmallow for 20 seconds to incorporate them. Pour the strawberry marshmallow over the vanilla marshmallow and smooth it into an even layer. Let the marshmallow sit and rest, undisturbed, at room temperature until it is completely set, about 8 hours.

When you're ready to cut the marshmallow, dust your work surface with the powdered sugar, and sprinkle a layer of powdered sugar on top of the marshmallow. Flip the marshmallow facedown onto the work surface and peel the foil or plastic wrap off the back. Dust a large chef's knife with powdered sugar and cut the marshmallow into long thin strips, cleaning the knife frequently as it gets sticky. Cut the strips of marshmallow into small squares. Toss the marshmallow squares in powdered sugar to prevent them from sticking together. Store the marshmallows in an airtight container at room temperature for up to 2 weeks.

Passion Fruit Marshmallows

YIELD: 1½ POUNDS (681 G)

10 ounces or 1¼ cups (295 ml) cold water, divided

4¼ ounces or ½ cup (119 g) passion fruit pulp, strained

1 ounce (28 g) or 4 (¼-ounce, or 7-g) envelopes unflavored gelatin

1 pound 5 ounces or 3 cups (588 g) granulated sugar

13¾ ounces or 1¼ cups (385 g) light corn syrup

Yellow and orange food coloring

2⅔ ounces or ⅔ cup (75 g) powdered sugar

Line a 9 x 13-inch (23 x 33-cm) baking pan with aluminum foil or plastic wrap, and spray the foil or plastic wrap with nonstick cooking spray.

Combine ½ cup (120 ml) of the water and the passion fruit pulp in the bowl of a large stand mixer. Sprinkle the gelatin over the top and whisk it into the liquid.

Combine the remaining ¾ cup (180 ml) water, the granulated sugar, and the light corn syrup in a medium saucepan. Stir to dissolve the sugar, and brush down the sides of the pan with a wet pastry brush to prevent crystals from forming. Place the pan over medium-high heat and insert a candy thermometer.

Cook the sugar syrup without stirring until it reaches 245°F (118°C) on the candy thermometer. The hot sugar syrup now needs to be added to the gelatin. If your saucepan does not have a spout, pour the syrup into a large mixing cup or pitcher with a spout, to give you more control over the process. Turn the mixer to low, and with the mixer running, slowly stream the hot sugar syrup into the gelatin. Try to pour the syrup close to the sides of the bowl, so it doesn't hit the whisk and splatter everywhere.

Once all of the syrup is added to the mixing bowl, gradually increase the speed of the mixer until it is running on medium-high speed. Whip the marshmallow until it is very thick, shiny, and opaque, about 8 to 10 minutes, depending on your mixer. When you lift the whisk from the marshmallow, it should slowly stream from the whisk in a thick ribbon. Add a few drops of yellow and orange food coloring, to give the marshmallow a light orange color, and stir them in.

(continued on next page)

Pour the marshmallow into the prepared pan and smooth it into an even layer. Let the marshmallow sit and rest, undisturbed, at room temperature until it is completely set, about 8 hours.

When you're ready to cut the marshmallow, dust your work surface with the powdered sugar, and sprinkle a layer of powdered sugar on top of the marshmallow. Flip the marshmallow facedown onto the work surface and peel the foil or plastic wrap off the back. Dust a large chef's knife with powdered sugar and cut the marshmallow into long thin strips, cleaning the knife frequently as it gets sticky. Cut the strips of marshmallow into small squares. Toss the marshmallow squares in powdered sugar to prevent them from sticking together. Store the marshmallows in an airtight container at room temperature for up to 2 weeks.

—

VARIATIONS: You can substitute other fruit purées for the passion fruit in this recipe. Mango, peach, strawberry, or raspberry (strained of seeds) all work very well and can be substituted on a 1:1 basis.

S'mores S'prises

7 rectangular graham cracker sheets, divided

12 ounces (336 g) dark chocolate, melted and tempered (see page 24)

24 (1-inch, or 2.5-cm) marshmallows (about 11 ounces, or 308 g)

Crumble 1 graham cracker into small pieces and set it aside for now.

Carefully cut the remaining 6 graham crackers along the scored lines to produce small rectangles, then cut each rectangle in half to form a 1-inch (2.5-cm) square. You will end up with 48 small graham squares.

Dab a little tempered chocolate on the top and bottom of a marshmallow, and press a graham cracker square on each side, forming a sandwich. Repeat until all of the marshmallows have been sandwiched between 2 crackers.

Dip the candy in the tempered chocolate, then set it on a parchment-lined counter to firm up. While the chocolate is still wet, sprinkle the tops of the S'mores S'prises with a pinch of the reserved crushed graham cracker. Store S'mores S'prises in an airtight container at room temperature for up to 2 weeks.

CHAPTER 11

Finishing Techniques and Candy Decorations

There is a saying in the culinary world that "you eat with your eyes." Visual presentation has a powerful impact when it comes to the food we choose to consume. Even the most delicious caramel will be passed over if it is dipped in gray, streaky bloomed chocolate, while a mediocre truffle is easily forgiven if it is covered with glossy chocolate and a picture-perfect pinch of nuts on top. Of course, good flavor should always be the primary goal of candy making, but once you have mastered a recipe's technique, the next step should be to present the candy as beautifully as possible.

Five Easy Truffle Decorations

Truffle decorations don't have to be limited to a roll in cocoa powder or a sprinkle of chopped nuts on top. These five simple decorating ideas require only a little time and effort, but they give your truffles a big personality. For instructions on how to dip truffles and prepare them for decorating, see page 90-92.

Spiked Truffles

Spiked truffles have an unexpected, refreshingly modern look. To finish your truffles this way, place a freshly dipped truffle on a cooling rack with a close-spaced wire grid pattern. Use a fork or dipping tools to roll the wet truffle around in circles on top of the rack. As the chocolate starts to set, some of it will stick to the rack, resulting in a rough, spiked surface all over the truffle. Roll it until it is evenly spiked on all sides, then transfer it to a sheet of parchment paper to set completely while you roll and spike other truffles **(A)**.

Dipping Tool Decorations

Dipping tools are good for more than just dipping truffles—they can also be used to create designs on top of the dipped chocolates. Touch the top of a freshly dipped truffle with the tines of a dipping tool to create swirls or lines on your truffles **(B, C)**.

Chocolate Swirls

To create fanciful swirls on top of your truffles, temper chocolate or melt candy coating in a contrasting color. Dip a fork into the melted chocolate and quickly flick it in circles over the truffles. Vary your movements and direction so that the pattern is random and unpredictable **(D)**.

Chocolate Stripes

Stripes are a clean and classic truffle decoration. To make stripes, pour tempered chocolate or melted candy coating into a paper cone or a pastry bag fitted with a small round tip. Gently squeeze the bag to release the chocolate while quickly moving the bag back and forth over the truffles. Let the chocolate set, then cut off any stray lines that have formed near the bottom of the truffle with a paring knife **(E)**.

Chocolate Designs

Don't limit yourself to stripes or swirls—use your truffles as a blank canvas and draw shapes, letters, or words on top. Pour tempered choco-

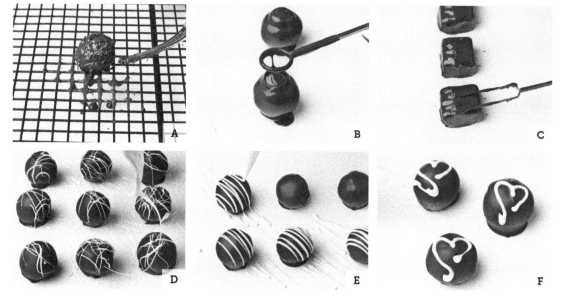

A. Spiked Truffles

B + C. Dipping Tool Decorations

D. Chocolate Swirls

E. Chocolate Stripes

F. Chocolate Designs

A. From left to right: disco dust, luster dust, sparkle dust, pearl dust, petal dust

B + C. Applying Dry Decoration Dust

D, E, F. Painting with Decorating Dust

late or melted candy coating into a paper cone or a pastry bag fitted with a small round tip, and practice a few times on parchment before you attempt drawing on top of a truffle, to make sure the chocolate flows well and you are comfortable with your design. **(F)**

Decorating Dusts

If you want to create beautiful sparkling candies with metallic or pearlescent finishes, decorating dusts are your new best friend. **(A)** These edible dusts come in small bottles and can be brushed on finished candies with a dry brush or mixed with cocoa butter and painted on. There are many different varieties of decorating dust, but here are the most common:

Disco dust: has large, metallic grains, similar in appearance to glitter.

Luster dust: has a vibrant shine and comes in a wide variety of colors. Because it provides a good balance of shine and strong color, luster dust is the most common kind of decorating dust used to finish candies.

Sparkle dust: has larger grains than luster dust, and provides an iridescent shine and subtle color.

Pearl dust: is practically translucent, but can impart a small amount of color. It is generally used to provide a pearlescent finish.

Petal dust: is a matte powder, without any shine. It provides deep color and is most often used to paint realistic flowers.

Applying Dry Decorating Dust

To apply decorating dust to your candies, use a clean, dry paintbrush. Decorating dust does not mix well with water and will clump together if it gets wet. Dip the brush in the dust and gently apply a thin, even layer to the top of your can-

dy. Decorating dust can be used on chocolates, truffles, hard candies, or any other confection that is smooth and dry. **(B)**

Decorating dust will rub off of the candy, so be careful when you handle, store, and package the finished candies. If any dust rubs off, it can easily be reapplied with a dry brush. **(C)**

Painting with Decorating Dust

In cake decorating, decorating dust is often mixed with alcohol to form a thin, smooth liquid that can be easily used for painting. Unfortunately, this method doesn't work on chocolates, but there is an alternative. If you mix melted cocoa butter and luster dust, you can form a colorful, shiny, chocolate-friendly paint. This method is best for adding small details to your candies, if you want to show texture or visible brushstrokes, or if you need the decorations to be more durable.

To paint with luster dust, melt a small amount of cocoa butter. Stir in the luster dust a little bit at a time, stopping to check the color and consistency periodically until the color is strong enough. **(D)**

Use a small paintbrush to apply the colored cocoa butter to dry, smooth candies or chocolates. The cocoa butter will gradually start to set at room temperature, so periodically warm it up in the microwave until it is fluid again. **(E)**

When your chocolates are complete, let the cocoa butter dry completely. Because the cocoa butter helps seal in the color, this painting method is less delicate and prone to scratching than dry-brushed luster dust, but you should still take care when handling and storing painted candies. **(F)**

Edible Gold Leaf

Edible gold leaf adds an authentic metallic sheen that is unmatched by any other product. As its name suggests, it is made from genuine gold, and is sold in either sheets or flakes. The flakes are convenient for sprinkling on top of candies, but the sheets offer more decorating versatility. When selecting gold leaf, make sure that it is between 22 and 24 karats—any less and it might contain impurities that make it unsafe to consume.

Gold leaf is extremely delicate and is easily torn or wrinkled. When handling gold leaf, wear cotton gloves if possible, and avoid touching it with your bare hands, as it will stick to the oil on your fingers. Try not to breathe heavily or move suddenly, because even a stray gust of wind can blow the gold leaf away or cause it to crumple. In addition to gold leaf, you will need a sharp paring knife or razor blade and a soft, dry paintbrush. **(A)**

Use the knife or razor blade to cut away a small portion of the gold leaf. Pick it up using the tip of your blade, and gently lift it up from the rest of the gold leaf. **(B)**

Position the gold leaf over the candy and set it down so that it attaches to the top of the candy and detaches from the blade. **(C)**

Use the paintbrush to carefully press down on the gold leaf and smooth it out, creating an even gold patch on the candy. **(D)**

If desired, you can repeat this process to add more gold leaf decorations to the top of your candy. If you want to cover the entire candy with gold leaf,

A   B   C

D   E   F

you can either use a much larger patch of gold leaf initially or overlap many individual pieces of gold leaf to make a seamless gold coating. **(E)**

Once your gold leaf candies are finished, handle them carefully, because the gold leaf can easily be rubbed or scratched off the surface. **(F)**

A

Chocolate Transfer Sheets

Chocolate transfer sheets are thin sheets of acetate covered with designs made from cocoa butter. When the sheets come into contact with melted chocolate, the cocoa butter pattern transfers to the chocolate's surface, resulting in beautiful, polished chocolate decorations. **(A)**

To decorate your chocolates with transfer sheets, you need to use chocolate candies with a flat surface. Square truffles or chocolate-dipped caramels are ideal for this purpose. Cut the transfer sheets into small squares that are slightly larger than the dipped candies. Dip your candies following the instructions on page 92, and while the chocolate is still wet, gently place a transfer sheet square on the candy. Make sure the rough side, with the cocoa powder design, is facedown on the chocolate. **(B)**

B

Use your finger or a small offset spatula to smooth the transfer sheet onto the top of the chocolate. Be sure to get all the way to the edges and corners. **(C)**

C

Let the chocolate set completely at room temperature. Once set, grasp the edge of the transfer sheet and carefully peel it back, leaving an elegant pattern on your candies. **(D)**

D

Molded Caramels

Caramels are most typically cut into squares or rectangles, but that doesn't mean you can't have some fun with this classic candy! Instead of sticking with staid shapes, use a candy mold to form your caramels and give them a whimsical touch. (A)

A

To create caramel shapes, you will need a silicone mold—regular plastic candy molds are not flexible enough to release the caramels. You can use a mold specifically designed for chocolate and candy making, or you can use a silicone ice cube tray. Ice cube trays are a fraction of the price of traditional silicone molds, they come in fun shapes, and they work just as well as the specialty chocolate molds.

Use one of the caramel recipes in chapter 5. A caramel that is cooked to a firm consistency is easier to mold than a soft caramel. After the caramel is cooked but while it is still liquid, pour or spoon the caramel into the cavities of your mold. **(B)**

B

Let the caramels cool to room temperature, then refrigerate the mold until the caramels are completely set and firm. Once set, turn the mold upside down and press the caramels out through the back of the mold. Dip them in chocolate or individually wrap and refrigerate them so that they hold their shape. **(C)**

C

Marshmallow Rosettes

Light and fluffy marshmallows look extra sweet when they're piped into rosette shapes with colorful swirls. This is a fun way to dress up your marshmallows for gifting and special occasions like showers and parties. **(A)**

Fit a pastry bag with a large star tip with an opening is at least ¾ inch (2 cm) wide. To create stripes, take a clean paintbrush and paint lines of gel food coloring up the inside of the bag. Fill the bag with freshly made marshmallow, using one of the recipes from chapter 10. Twist the bag closed at the top. **(B)**

Cover a baking sheet with parchment, and sprinkle a layer of granulated sugar onto the parchment. Holding the bag upright, squeeze the pastry bag to press the marshmallow out onto the baking sheet, and as it comes out, move the bag in a circle to make a rosette shape. Once you've completed a circle, stop squeezing and lift the bag up, to break off the tip of the rosette. (C)

While the marshmallow rosettes are still wet, sprinkle the tops with a light coating of granulated sugar. Let the marshmallows set completely at room temperature, for at least 6 hours or overnight. Once set, store the rosettes in an airtight container at room temperature between layers of waxed paper. **(D)**

Custom Candy Molds

Candy molds are convenient, but they can be limiting. It can be hard to find molds in your desired shapes or sizes, and sometimes you might want to mold candies, like marshmallows or fondant, that are difficult to shape using traditional candy or chocolate molds. The solution to this problem is to make your own custom molds out of cornstarch.

This section shows how to make marshmallow eggs in a cornstarch mold, but cornstarch molds don't have to be limited to marshmallows—they can also be used to mold hard candies, gumdrops, jelly candies, and melted fondant. **(A)**

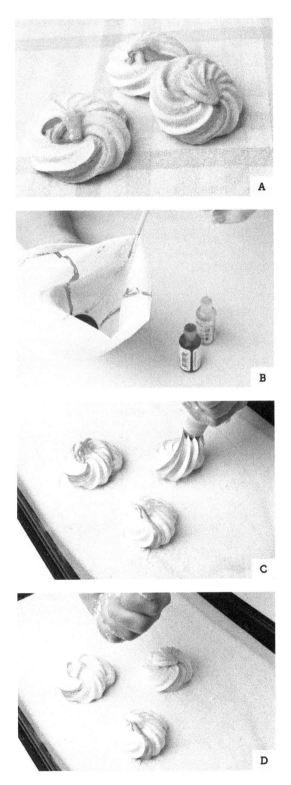

A

B

C

D

To make a cornstarch mold, sift cornstarch into a 9 x 13-inch (23 x 33-cm) pan or a half-sheet pan. The choice of pan depends on how many cavities you need and how deep your cavities will be. Plan on using about 4 to 5 pounds 1.8 to 2.3 kg) of cornstarch for a 9 x 13-inch (23 x 33-cm) pan or a half-sheet pan. **(B)**

Use a ruler or straightedge to level the top of the cornstarch until it is completely even and smooth. **(C)**

Press your shape of choice into the cornstarch. Virtually anything can be used to create these molds—a kitchen tool, like a utensil or the bottom of a cup or bowl, a household object, a toy, or a piece of jewelry can all produce an interesting shape. Press down firmly to make a solid impression, and be sure to leave enough space between the shapes so that the cornstarch does not collapse in on itself. **(D)**

Pipe or pour your candy into the cavities. Hard candies and liquid fondant can be poured into the holes, while marshmallows should be carefully piped in to fill up all available space. **(E)**

Sift a light layer of cornstarch on top of the candy, and let it set completely at room temperature. **(F)**

Once the candy is set, gently remove the pieces from the cornstarch. Use a pastry brush to brush off the excess cornstarch. The cornstarch from the mold can be reused to make more molds. **(G)**

Chocolate Bowls

YIELD: 16 CHOCOLATE BOWLS

1 pound (454 g) chocolate, melted, tempered (see page 24)

16 small, round water balloons

Inflate the small, round water balloons. Do not over-inflate—they should remain flexible and have some "give" to them. Dip the bottom of a balloon into the chocolate until it is the height you desire. Spin the balloon around in the chocolate to make sure it is the same height on all sides. **(A)** Gently place the balloon down on a piece of parchment, holding it upright until the chocolate forms a small foot and can stand on its own without tipping over. **(B)** Let the chocolate set completely at room temperature.

To remove the balloon from the chocolate bowl, carefully squeeze the sides of the balloon to break the seal all the way around the bowl. **(C)** Pinch the top of the balloon under the knot, and snip a hole in the knot above your fingers. **(D)** Keep your fingers tightly closed so that you control the flow of air out of the balloon. **(E)**

Slowly relax your grip, letting the air out of the balloon gradually. If you do this too fast, the chocolate can crack or the balloon will become stuck to the sides of the bowl. If the balloon deflates slowly, it will gently peel itself from the inside of the chocolate bowl. Once the balloon is completely deflated, carefully peel it from the bottom of the chocolate bowl. **(F)**

Store these Chocolate Bowls in an airtight container at cool room temperature for up to a month.

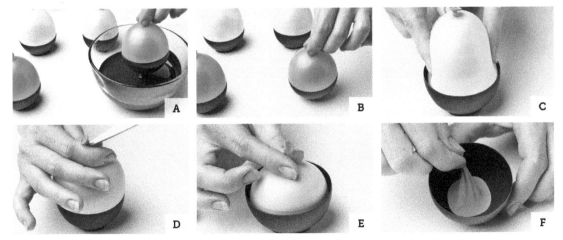

Spun Sugar

2 ounces or ¼ cup (60 ml) water

2¾ ounces or ¼ cup (77 g) light corn syrup

14 ounces or 2 cups (392 g) granulated sugar

Ice

In a 2-quart (1.8-L) saucepan, combine the water, corn syrup, and granulated sugar, and place the pan over medium-high heat. Stir until the sugar dissolves, then brush down the sides of the pan with a wet pastry brush. Bring the syrup to a boil, and once boiling, insert a candy thermometer.

Continue to cook the candy, without stirring, until it reaches 310°F (154°C) on the candy thermometer. While the candy cooks, combine the ice and some cold water in a bowl to form an ice bath, and arrange several saucepan handles, dowels, or rolling pins over a countertop covered with parchment paper.

Once the sugar reaches 310°F (154°C), remove the pan from the heat and dunk the bottom of the pan in the bowl of ice water to stop it from cooking. **(A)** Remove the pan from the ice water and let it cool at room temperature for several minutes, until it has thickened enough to form a thin strand of sugar.

Dip a fork or wire whisk with the ends cut off into the cooked sugar, and, holding it 12 inches (30 cm) above the countertop, flick it quickly back and forth over the saucepan handles. **(B)** Continue to dip and flick the whisk until you have as much spun sugar as you need.

Gently gather it together in your hands. You can keep it one long strand, divide it into smaller portions and fashion it into a ring, or roll it over your fingers to make a ball of spun sugar. **(C)** This decoration is extremely delicate and sensitive to humidity. Spun sugar should be used within a few hours after making it.

A B C

Bubble Sugar

2⅔ ounces or ⅓ cup (80 ml) water

1½ ounces or 2 tablespoons (42 g) light corn syrup

7 ounces or 1 cup (196 g) granulated sugar

1½ tablespoons (22 ml) vodka

In a small saucepan, combine the water, corn syrup, and granulated sugar, and place the pan over medium-high heat. **(A)** Stir until the sugar dissolves, then brush down the sides of the pan with a wet pastry brush to prevent sugar crystals from forming. Bring the syrup to a boil, and once boiling, insert a candy thermometer. **(B)**

Continue to cook the candy, without stirring, until it reaches 310°F (154°C) on the candy thermometer. While you wait for the candy to reach the proper temperature, prepare a piece of parchment paper by crumpling it between your hands. **(C)** Smooth the parchment out onto a rimmed baking sheet—it should still retain some of the wrinkles and texture. Hold the baking sheet at an angle and drizzle the vodka over the top of the parchment so that it runs down and covers the paper. **(D)**

Once the candy reaches 310°F (154°C), remove the pan from the heat. Hold the baking sheet at an angle and carefully pour the hot sugar syrup onto the parchment, so that it flows down the paper. The vodka on the crinkled paper will cause the sugar to bubble, forming a delicate, lacy texture. **(E)**

Let the sugar cool and harden completely at room temperature. Once cool, flip it upside down and carefully peel off the parchment from the back of the bubble sugar. **(F)** Break the sugar into small pieces by hand and use it to decorate cakes and pastries. Bubble sugar is sensitive to moisture, so it should be used on the day it is made. Do not store it in the refrigerator or any humid environment.

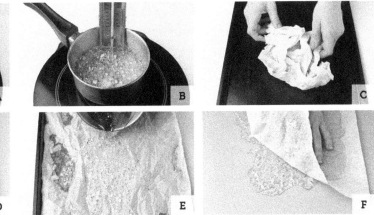

Sugar Spirals

¼ teaspoon fresh lemon juice

7 ounces or 1 cup (196 g) granulated sugar

Rub the lemon juice into the sugar until it is well distributed and the sugar is slightly damp from the juice. **(A)** This will help prevent crystallization when you caramelize the sugar.

Place a small pan over medium heat and let it preheat for several minutes until the pan is hot. Add the sugar, and begin to stir immediately and continuously. **(B)** Continue to cook the sugar, stirring constantly, until it liquefies. **(C)** Shortly after it becomes liquid it will start to color. Cook the caramel until it is a medium amber color. **(D)**

When you first take the caramel off the heat, it will be thin and fluid. **(E)** As it continues to cook in the pan and cool, it will become darker and thicker. Let the caramel sit at room temperature until it forms a thick ribbon and gives some resistance when you scoop up a spoonful from the pan. **(F)**

Lightly oil a round knife sharpener or the round metal handle of a spoon. Hold the sharpener in one hand and scoop up a spoonful of thickened caramel in the other. Let most of the caramel drop off the spoon back into the pan, and when you have just a thin strand hanging from the spoon, begin to wind it around the oiled sharpener, beginning at the handle. **(G)** If it drips from the sharpener to the counter, the caramel is still too thin and needs to cool for a few more minutes.

Continue to wind the sugar around the sharpener until you reach the end. Let it cool for just a moment, then gently break off any hanging strands and carefully slide the spiral off the sharpener. **(H)** You can vary the speed of your movements and the temperature of the sugar to make spirals of different thicknesses: warmer caramel and faster movements produce very thin spirals, while colder caramel and slow movements make thicker, darker spirals.

Sugar spirals should be enjoyed on the same day they are made, and should not be stored in a humid environment.

Resources

Here is a list of online resources for finding candy ingredients, supplies, and kitchen equipment.

Molds, Flavorings, Colorings, and General Candy-Making Supplies for Home Kitchens

Candyland Crafts
www.candylandcrafts.com
Candy packaging, flavoring oils, candy molds, tempering machines

Country Kitchen SweetArt
www.countrykitchensa.com
Candy molds, candy coating, decorating dust, prepared candy centers

Jesters Discount Cake Supply
www.lusterdust.com
Large variety and selection of decorating dusts

KitchenKrafts
www.kitchenkrafts.com
Decorating tools, candy molds, chocolate, and candy coating

SugarCraft
www.sugarcraft.com
Candy flavorings and colorings, invertase, cocoa butter

Wilton
www.wilton.com
Decorating and dipping tools (also available at many arts and craft stores)

Professional Candy-Making Supplies and Equipment

Chef Rubber
www.chefrubber.com
Transfer sheets, fine chocolates, citric acid, invertase, gold leaf

JB Prince
www.jbprince.com
Silicone molds, tempering machines, packaging and accessories

Pastry Chef Central
www.pastrychef.com
Scales, thermometers, professional tools, gold leaf

Tomric Systems
www.tomric.com
High-quality chocolate molds, professional tools, tempering machines

Gourmet Chocolates

Chocolate Source
www.chocolatesource.com

Chocosphere
www.chocosphere.com

Gourmail
www.gourmail.com

Specialty Ingredients

Amazon
www.amazon.com
Pomona's Universal Pectin, citric acid, vanilla bean paste

Culinary District
www.culinarydistrict.com
Vanilla bean paste, citric acid, almond paste, specialty chocolates

Nuts.com
www.nuts.com
Freeze-dried fruit, fresh nuts, tart dried cherries

About the Author

Elizabeth LaBau is a food writer, a recipe developer, and an enthusiastic candy eater. A former pastry chef, she uses her years of experience working in professional kitchens to bring a modern touch to the world of old-fashioned candy making. Since 2006, she has been the Guide to Candy at About.com, an online division of the New York Times Company, where she writes creative candy recipes and step-by-step tutorials for the home cook. When Elizabeth is not playing with sugar in the kitchen, she can be found running the mountain trails around Los Angeles with a piece of candy tucked into her pocket. Learn more at www.sugarhero.com.

Index

CPSIA information can be obtained
at www.ICGtesting.com
Printed in the USA
BVHW020514110522
636527BV00002B/2